LEARNING
TO TEACH

TEACHER PREPARATION
IN VICTORIA, BC
1903-1963

Vernon Storey

The Bradley Project

LEARNING TO TEACH

TEACHER PREPARATION
IN VICTORIA, BC
1903-1963

First Edition

Published by **The Bradley Project** at the Faculty of Education,
University of Victoria, Box 3010, Victoria BC, V8W 3N4

The Bradley Project was established in 2003 to aid in
disseminating materials relating to the history of teacher education
in British Columbia, initially through the publication of this book.
The publisher of record is the Faculty of Education,
University of Victoria.

Illustrations from University of Victoria Archives and Special
Collections and from individuals, attributed where known.

Design by ThomasDesign, Victoria, BC

Cover image adapted from Camosun College website.

Printed in Canada

Canadian Cataloguing in Publication Data

Storey, Vernon J. (Vernon James), 1943

Learning to teach: Teacher preparation in Victoria, BC 1903-1963

Includes bibliographical references.

ISBN 1-55058-269-0

Table of Contents

LEARNING
TO TEACH

TEACHER PREPARATION
IN VICTORIA, BC
1903-1963

Dedication

PERCIVAL E. WILKINSON

More than symbolically, Percy ("Wilkie") Wilkinson's 100th birthday on July 1, 2003 represents this book's purpose – to capture the story of an important era in the development of post-secondary education in British Columbia. For many years since he completed his qualifying year at Victoria Provincial Normal School in 1926-27, Percy has been a tireless advocate of first the establishment and subsequently the growth and development of the University of Victoria.

Percy was born in Oregon and at the age of five moved with his parents to southern Vancouver Island, where he grew up in Saanich and Victoria. He was taught by his parents at home for about five years, then attended elementary school at Saanichton and Monterey and completed high school through McGill University junior matriculation courses at Sprott-Shaw School, which itself celebrated its 100th anniversary in 2003. He soon realized that he would need further education "if I was ever going to do anything with my life." With that in mind, Percy embarked on a journey that included university correspondence and summer sessions at UBC for his B.A. degree (1935). Part of his effort was financed by washing dishes in a lumber camp. Percy's B.Ed. degree (1958) from the University of British Columbia further identified him as what he had long been – a teacher.

Percy has been a teacher among teachers: organizing reunions of his Normal School class, keeping his friendships with colleagues who remain, advocating higher education, and supporting the work of the University of Victoria as a proud alumnus from the early years of its history. He worked for many years in the Department of Education, with responsibilities for examinations and for teacher certification until his retirement in 1969.

Speaking in his biographical notes of an extension in that position, Percy observed "On the basis of my age, I should have retired at the end of July 1968." As I conversed with him on several occasions during the writing of this book, and as I heard his lively address to the Annual General Meeting of the University of Victoria Alumni Association on June 11, 2003, I realized that in some important ways, Percy Wilkinson still had not retired. I am grateful to him both for his commitment to education in its broadest sense and for his assistance with this book. Percy stands as a worthy representative of those who over many years have chosen teaching as their career.

Percival E. ("Wilkie") Wilkinson, 2003
Photograph courtesy of Jenus Friesen,
photographer.

LEARNING TO TEACH

TEACHER PREPARATION
IN VICTORIA, BC
1903-1963

Preface

The Faculty of Education at the University of Victoria is a relatively young organization. It has been a member of that academic community since UVIC's 1963 opening. Yet like many other organizations, the Faculty finds its roots in other names, in other locations, and in earlier years than its life of the past 40 years suggests.

The Faculty's mission statement clarifies its present role as a broadly based, comprehensive unit within the University:

The Faculty of Education is committed to the education and development of professionals in a broad spectrum of educational settings within a context of lifelong learning. The Faculty will advance educational thought and research, model exemplary practice, seek, generate and disseminate knowledge and provide professional service in the fields of education. It will strengthen its leadership position in the delivery of programs and research at the provincial, national and international levels.[1]

That stance marks a major metamorphosis from the days of the Victoria Provincial Normal School and its antecedent in Superintendent of Education John Jessop's 1872 examination to qualify teachers at the third class certificate level to teach in British Columbia's public schools. It also denotes a much broader approach than in Jessop's day, an emphasis on lifelong learning in a variety of contexts and a focus on the work of professionals who seek to guide others on that journey.

This book traces some of the steps and events from Jessop's determination that public school teachers should be certified to practice their craft, to the most recent major structural change. That latter remaking of the process of teacher education, the change that brought into being today's Faculty of Education, was the 1963 birth of the University of Victoria.

Post-secondary education in Victoria, British Columbia began in 1903. This book is about some of the people, events and developments from the first 60 years of that history, leading up to the establishment of the University of Victoria. Its particular focus is on the preparation of teachers during that period, a history now recalled by fewer among us, and on some of the events and stories that mark the journey. The book represents my effort to gather and to capture in print the account that has existed in archival records, in the stories of participants still present, and in the memorabilia preserved by them and their families and students. It seeks to honour those who taught British Columbia's public school pupils in earlier days and those from whom they learned about teaching.

Several dates mark key events along the route from teacher candidacy examinations to today's UVic Faculty of Education. In 1903, Victoria College (McGill) was established to offer, initially, first year university arts and science courses. As Peter Smith has noted, although this early venture was not designed specifically to prepare teachers:

> As far as we can tell, most young men and women who had completed available coursework at Victoria College proceeded at once to take elementary teaching jobs, either as a permanent career or as a temporary expedient to save money for further study.[2]

It would be several years until a program designed specifically to train teachers was established in Victoria. However, during the early days of Victoria College "the great majority...entered the teaching profession,[3]" even though there was no local preparation opportunity. A Provincial Normal School was established in Vancouver in 1901; a second opened in Victoria in 1915. That year, ending a dispute about where 'the' University for British Columbia would be located, the provincial government placed the campus in Vancouver and closed Victoria College, which was reopened in 1920. The College was housed in Victoria High School for a year before taking up longer term residence in Craigdarroch Castle in 1921. The Victoria Provincial Normal School remained in its new building on Lansdowne Road until 1942. That year, the building was turned over to the federal government for use as a military hospital until the end of World War II. In 1946, the building was restored to its former function, but with a difference. From that point until its closing in 1956 the Normal School would share its facility with Victoria College, which had been forced from its accommodation in Craigdarroch Castle by a lack of sufficient space.

In 1956, Victoria Provincial Normal School ceased operation as a separate entity in a merger with Victoria College, which by then was affiliated with the University of British Columbia. In 1958, Victoria College appointed Henry Gilliland, the last of the four Victoria Provincial Normal School principals, to chair the College's newly created Department of Teacher Education. That structure remained in place until 1963, when the University of Victoria commenced operation as an independent university. The former Victoria College is now Camosun College, a multi-program three-campus facility serving students on the southern end of Vancouver Island.

Somewhere along the way, the task of writing a book becomes an affair of the heart. What begins as a casual introduction to an idea, we discover, soon becomes a relationship - a full-blown, compelling, sometimes stormy connection between writer and writing. It is a mysterious business that marks the writing task with the complexities of a relationship that both invites departure and compels continuation. In the case of this book, a chance meeting became a committed relationship almost overnight.

In 2002, the University of Victoria was planning the following year's celebrations of its own 40th anniversary and the 100th anniversary of post-secondary education in the capital of British Columbia. Clearly, the University had a rich and vibrant history marked by significant events and stages in the story that began with the establishment of Victoria College (McGill) in 1903, followed by the 1915 opening of the Victoria Provincial Normal School. Those antecedents of the present UVic Faculty of Education represented important themes in the story of teacher preparation on southern Vancouver Island.

In May 2002, the Deans, Chairs, and Directors of the University of Victoria's Faculty of Education held a two-day meeting to review the Faculty's strategic plan in light of the overall plan for the University. The upcoming 2003 centennial celebrations emerged as a topic of discussion. The Faculty had just hosted a reception in recognition of the new Faculty of Education Chapter of the UVic Alumni Association. Alumni guests among the 200 or so who gathered for the occasion included Mr. Percy Wilkinson, a graduate of the Victoria Provincial Normal School class of 1927, and Mrs. Joyce Flett, who spoke of her experience as a member of the class of 1934-35. Clearly, this early Chapter event was an occasion for the Faculty to remember. These alumni were part of an important sequence in the development of teacher education in British Columbia, a foundational story that needed to be captured and preserved.

I had recently completed a project as one of the authors of another historical book, *The Home: From Orphans' Home to Family Centre 1873 to 1998.* [4] I was struck by the parallels. Each of these two institutions had carried for many years its own strong mandate on behalf of children and their families. Each was reaching an important milestone - for the Cridge Centre a 125th anniversary, for the Faculty a major part in celebrating the centenary of post-secondary education on southern Vancouver Island. Each carried an important social responsibility to recognize the people for whom the institution had represented an important period in their lives - the children of the Orphans' Home and the soon-to-become teachers of the Victoria Provincial Normal School. One of those stories had now been recorded in a book; the other awaited that step.

Archivists use the term *ephemera* to describe the objects and scraps of text that offer tiny clues and fleeting glimpses into lives and events. Unfortunately, ephemera offer little on which to build a fuller history. My concern was that the story of the early days of teacher education in Victoria ran the risk of becoming ephemeral, surviving only as scattered accounts within the broader history of teacher education and of British Columbia.

My early inquiries had suggested that a comprehensive set of office records from the Victoria Provincial Normal School might be difficult if not impossible to locate. Further, the size of the group who had been part of those early days was dwindling with the passage of time. To delay the project could mean losing the possibility of access to these people, their stories, and the records and memorabilia they might be willing to share. I decided to explore the possibility of writing a book that would capture a portion of the record in time for the 2003 celebrations.

I am not a historian in the sense that the Oxford Dictionary speaks of "a person learned in history." My background is that of a teacher, principal and school superintendent, and more recently, a professor of leadership studies at the University of Victoria. *The Home*, to which Terry Worobetz and Henry Kennedy were important co-contributors, was my first venture into writing about people and events from before my own time. However, it was apparent to me that if our history is to offer accounts of human experience for those who follow and who seek to make some sense of their past, those accounts must be preserved. In this case, it was important also to juxtapose the local history of teacher education with the development of the University of Victoria. That history involves several organizational names, structural changes, and a variety of locales. It stretches over a 100-year period that began just 60 years after James Douglas' arrival on the southern tip of Vancouver Island as a representative of the Hudson's Bay Company.

I have sought to capture to the extent possible the flavour of the times - the thought of the day, as expressed by those who contributed to the official record through their correspondence and reports. They included members of the civil service and other government officials; teachers who corresponded with their colleagues, and other citizens who recalled and shared their own experiences. Some of the quotations I have used are lengthy, because recasting these ideas in the words of another might have meant sacrificing some of the meaning, nuance, and emphasis intended by the original writers. Where I have edited interviewees' stories for structural reasons, I have followed a fairly straightforward and minimal process. I have simply deleted some of the natural redundancy of oral conversation while seeking to preserve essential meanings and intents.

This book owes much to a large number of individuals: staff members of the University of Victoria Archives and Special Collections; the Victoria College Craigdarroch Castle Alumni Association; Archives of the Anglican Church, Diocese of British Columbia; and the British Columbia Archives; my graduate assistant Ann Beck, who spent many productive, sometimes frustrating hours searching the historical record; Yesman Post for her analysis of the roots of the normal school movement; Lona McRae for her careful proofreading in search of the elusive last error; Laurel Regan for searching out a vital photograph; Dr. Mary Harker for her recollections of her friend and mentor Dr. Henrietta Anderson, and especially the Victoria Provincial Normal School graduates from 1927 to 1956 who so enthusiastically shared their stories of the short but intense preparation year that was pivotal in their journey toward becoming teachers in the schools of British Columbia. That group, especially its membership from the earlier years, is growing smaller as time passes. Their stories are representative of many hundreds of similar Victoria Provincial Normal School students' accounts. Some preferred to remain anonymous; I have honoured those requests. The stories were rich; the memories were clear; the feelings were often poignant. Several who expressed concern that they would have little to contribute in fact were able to enrich the account greatly through their personal recollections. Almost all remembered their Normal School days fondly; many had returned for one or more of the class reunions held over the years. These teachers were pioneers in the journey from an experiment that began as normal school and progressed to today's university-based program of teacher education. Regrettably, these stories are fewer in number than I might have preferred, and I have not touched on the experiences of former VPNS faculty members. The latter I leave for another writer.

Finally, I am deeply appreciative of the tangible support from several sources that enabled publication of this book. I gratefully acknowledge the financial support of the Province of British Columbia through the Ministry of Education. The project was also supported financially by the University of Victoria Alumni Association and by the Faculty of Education, University of Victoria. The financial and other support provided by each of these agencies has ensured that an account of the early history of teacher education in British Columbia, and particularly in Victoria, will be preserved as part of the record of human endeavour in this westernmost province of Canada.

Vernon Storey

Notes to Preface

[1] University of Victoria Faculty of Education, *The World of Learning: A Strategic Plan and Vision for the Faculty of Education* (Victoria: University of Victoria, 2002), 3.

[2] Peter L. Smith, *A Multitude of the Wise; UVic Remembered* (Victoria, BC: Alumni Association of the University of Victoria, 1993), 38.

[3] Ibid., 42.

[4] Vernon Storey, Henry Kennedy, and Terry Worobetz, *The Home: Orphans' Home to Family Centre, 1873 to 1998* (Victoria, BC: Cridge Centre for the Family, 1999).

LEARNING
TO TEACH
TEACHER PREPARATION
IN VICTORIA, BC
1903-1963

Chapter One
The Founding Years

The vocation of teaching the mind and the mission of caring for the soul have often been intertwined in social history. Both were evident from the early days of the arrival of European strangers on southern Vancouver Island. The Hudson's Bay Company had established its local presence in 1843 with the arrival of its agent James Douglas, who immediately constructed Fort Victoria to advance and protect the Company's interests. Fort Victoria's first school teacher was the Reverend John Staines, briefly chaplain to the Hudson's Bay Company. Staines, who arrived with his wife and nephew in 1849, was immediately assigned the job of schoolmaster along with the performance of his clerical duties. He was later described in the reminiscences of one of the Fort's pupils as "a good teacher with a somewhat uncertain temper."[1] Hudson's Bay Company governor James Douglas at first considered Staines a beneficial influence, but the pastor-teacher soon fell from favor because of his agitation against the Company's administrative policies. Douglas dismissed John Staines from the post of schoolmaster in 1854.

That year, Staines left the colony with a list of grievances, intending to return to England and report his concerns to the Company. He unfortunately drowned when the ship capsized off Cape Flattery early in the voyage. The company began the search for a new chaplain, finding one in the person of Reverend Edward Cridge, who arrived from England with his teacher wife Mary in 1855. The couple began a long association with Church, school, and young people – particularly, orphaned and deserted children. Reverend Cridge quickly became both prominent and popular in Fort Victoria, seen by some as Victoria's first social worker and, with Mary, a founder of services to the area's suffering and less privileged. Edward Cridge's portrait, cello in hand, is displayed today in the lobby of Victoria's Royal Jubilee Hospital. He was appointed Superintendent of Education without pay until 1865, when Alfred Waddington took over the position. During those early years, religious orders such as the Sisters of Saint Anne were also carrying out the work of teaching on southern Vancouver Island and elsewhere in what would soon become British Columbia.

Within a few years, the young province established a nonsectarian public school system to address the challenge of schooling children in a vast region that as yet was sparsely populated. Distances were great, transportation was difficult, the terrain was formidable, and priorities were conflicted. This was a community struggling to establish itself in the context of an unfamiliar land to which its European settlers had not been invited. Its stories are many; this book focuses on one small collection of those accounts. It traces the early development of British Columbia's schools and the preparation of teachers for those schools, focusing particularly on the latter in Victoria and at the Victoria Provincial Normal School.

A Public School System

The struggles of settlement and the fever of a gold rush assumed priority over the work of teachers in those early years. Though some of the teachers in local schools and in others west of the prairies had received formal preparation for their craft, they certainly had not acquired it locally. Clearly, though, there was from the beginning a government concern for teacher qualification and formal licensing to practice. That concern was captured in two documents of the early 1870s, the first piece of British Columbia schools legislation[2] and the first annual report on its fledgling public school system.[3] John Jessop, British Columbia's Superintendent of Education and a primary architect of the Province's early education legislation, had a hand in both documents. Bill 16, *An Act Respecting Public Schools*, made its way through the British Columbia Legislative Assembly in 1872, soon after the area was established as a Canadian province.

The first Act did not provide for a system of teacher preparation; that would emerge some 30 years later. However, the legislation did establish the broad outline of an organized system of schooling and recognized the need for at least the Province's senior officials to be licensed to teach. However, though the Act stated that the Superintendent of Education must be "an experienced and successful Teacher of at least five years' standing,"[4] it made no British Columbia-based provision either for his training or for that of any other teacher in the Province's school system. Instead the legislation acknowledged that the Superintendent would have to gain his qualifications elsewhere and present them in the form of "a first class certificate from some College, School, or Board of Examination in some other Province or Country where a Public School System has been in operation."[5]

Bill 16 established a Board of Education for the province and outlined its duties, among them the responsibility "to examine and give certificates of qualification to Teachers of Public Schools."[6] An Appendix to the Act recognized that this new system of public education was a work in progress, noting that for the moment teachers would be licensed through "the present temporary arrangement under which only third class certificates are granted."[7] Provision was made for first and second class certificates to be added later, but only "when the necessary formularies are more perfectly organized than at present."[8] For the moment, and for some years to follow, teacher certification would consist solely of candidates' successful completion of a set of written examination papers based largely on public school curriculum.

Jessop moved quickly to formalize the certification process. The first 18 candidates were examined in 1872; 13 were granted third class teaching certificates. Among this first group, the certificate of Mr. A. W. Rogers was initially "withheld as he not being sufficiently advanced in one branch; as, however, the South Cowichan School Trustees and people were anxious to secure his services as a Teacher, he was allowed further time, and qualified on 23rd July."[9] To achieve certification, candidates identified subjects "they may respectively consider themselves qualified to undertake; bearing in mind the standing of each as a scholar,"[10] and wrote examinations in those subjects.

Those first candidates for teacher certification chose from a list of examination subjects that included: Arithmetic, Geography, English Grammar, English History, Vocal Music, School

Organization and Government, and Composition.[11] Two points about that list are of particular interest. First, the list, which began with five examinations that could be referenced specifically to curricular areas, was interrupted by the insertion of "School Organization and Government." It concluded with a return to the curricular emphasis – Composition. Second, the Composition examination was the only one that posed different questions for male and female candidates.

Except for one question regarding the matter of a first school organizational assembly, the School Organization and Government examination of 1872 focused strongly on regulation and control, themes that were present in the legislation and would persist for many years in the organization, protocols, and expectations related to the teacher certification process. Order and orderliness were major concerns of the day, and that message was to be carried by the Province's teachers. The candidacy examination questions were explicit:

1. On what should obedience, particularly in young children, be based: and what expedients would you employ to produce it?

2. What principle should regulate rewards and punishments in school?

3. What do you consider the best means of attaining the following objects in school, namely:

    I. Securing attention;

    II. Securing order;

    III. Exciting interest in study.[12]

These questions reflected a sharp focus on the moral character and social deportment of students, an emphasis that was further evident in the Rules and Regulations for the Government of Public Schools accompanying Bill 16 (capitals in original):

(9) To observe and impress upon the minds of the pupils, the great rule of regularity and order, – A TIME AND PLACE FOR EVERYTHING, AND EVERYTHING IN ITS PROPER TIME AND PLACE.

(10) To promote, both by precept and example, CLEANLINESS, NEATNESS, AND DECENCY. To personally inspect the children every morning, to see that they have their hands and faces

washed, their hair combed, and clothes clean. The school apartments, too, should be swept and dusted every evening;

(11) To pay the strictest attention to the morals and general conduct of the pupils; to omit no opportunity of inculcating the principles of TRUTH and HONESTY; the duties of respect to superiors, and obedience to all persons placed in authority over them;

(12) to evince a regard for the improvement and general welfare of the pupils; to treat them with kindness, combined with firmness; and to aim at governing them by their affections and reason rather than harshness and severity;

(13) To cultivate kindly and affectionate feelings among the pupils; to discountenance quarrelling, cruelty to animals, and every approach to vice;[13]

Curiously, the Regulations tacitly acknowledged both a right of pupils and a restriction on the behaviour of teachers with a small insertion that addressed the matter of conflict of interest: "No Teacher shall compel the services of pupils for his own private benefit or convenience."[14]

The principle of *in loco parentis* also was foundational to the governance and regulation of British Columbia schools from the outset. Beginning with these early days, the parameters for discipline were made clear in a principle that has persisted for more than 100 years, even though its wording and application have changed over time: "To practice such discipline in School as would be exercised by a judicious parent in the family."[15] Those expectations and regulations, by inference, created some lasting expectations and norms for teachers in this frontier province's school system.

The second point of interest in regard to the 1872 examination to qualify for certification as a teacher relates to the last exam on the list. Candidates writing the Composition examination were assigned questions identified specifically for their sex: "*Males* – Influence of Canadian Pacific Railway on the future of British Columbia. *Females* – Write what you know of 'Dolly Varden'." One might speculate as to the reasons for different questions for men and women and for this specific selection of items. Clearly, the construction of the Canadian Pacific Railway represented a momentous development that probably was familiar to most of the general population, at least those who read the newspapers.

Developments related to the CPR were publicized widely in the country's newspapers over a considerable period. It might be reasonable to assume that many citizens, particularly those with substantially more formal education than their peers, would be able to offer comment about matters relating to the railway and its role in the development of Western Canada.

On the other hand, it seems unlikely that "Dolly Varden" would have enjoyed the same prominence. Today, many know Dolly Varden only as a species of brilliantly marked game fish. The term has been incorporated into the names and publicity materials of many wilderness fishing camps. At the time of the 1872 teacher candidate examinations, though, those acquainted with Dolly Varden probably would have known her as a character in Charles Dickens' *Barnaby Rudge*. She was described in one passage as "the very pink and pattern of good looks, in a smart little cherry-coloured mantle, with a hood of the same drawn over her head."[16] They may also have been familiar with the Gordon Riots of 1780 that provided a context for this work by Dickens – perhaps possession of that knowledge was an expectation of the examiners. One is left to speculate as to whether the questions might also have indicated an inherent gender bias on the part of the examiners. Certainly, a young woman unfamiliar with the works of Dickens would have found herself at a disadvantage if she had chosen Composition as an examination subject.

Even the existence of this mandatory examination process, though, was no assurance in the early years that all would comply with the minimal early effort to ensure duly licensed teachers. Noting a personnel problem at Craigflower School near Victoria just two years later, the Inspector acknowledged his frustration:

My hopes of improvement in this school – one of the most important in the Province, outside of the cities and towns – have not, I am sorry to say, been realized. The same want of attention to school work, carelessness with regard to the condition of the school house and its surroundings, negligence of personal appearance, and other habits quite incompatible with the proper discharge of his duties, still characterize the teacher. He has been holding the teachership in violation of the School Act since July, 1873, having declined to undergo an examination for two consecutive years. The educational interests of the children have been, and are still being, sacrificed to a desire, on the part of a few, to keep him in the school. A change in the teachership is absolutely necessary; and the sooner it takes place the better for all concerned.[17]

The challenges were not limited to the competence of teachers on southern Vancouver Island or in the province's nearer regions. British Columbia, a vast and only slightly explored region in the 1870s, was the ancestral home of many aboriginal nations and, very recently, the settling place of a few thousand European immigrants.

Geography and climate were natural adversaries of government, aided in their task by a pioneering and independent citizenry, many of whom probably saw the West as a place of potential freedom from the shackles of organized and regulated life. Most of the Province's school communities were tiny in population. In many cases, homes in an area were spread over considerable distance. School conflicts were not always resolved in ways that we might with hindsight assess as rational or cost-effective. However, the remedies in some cases were both original and creative. In his 1875 report to the Superintendent of Education, the Nicola Valley Inspector noted that:

It being found impossible to harmonize conflicting opinions as to where the school house should be located in this district . . . A compromise was effected by putting up one building above the large Indian reserve . . . and another below this Reserve . . . Both these school houses were completed in July last, and are comfortable and substantial little buildings, constructed with squared logs . . . the teacher . . . commenced an itinerant system of tuition, half-a-day in each school alternately, under very favourable auspices.[18]

Jessop's first Annual Report listed the names of all teachers appointed that year to work in British Columbia's fledgling public school system – about 30 in all.[19] Jessop also acknowledged 17 denominational and private schools in the province, 12 of them located in Victoria.[20]

The Superintendent conceded the current incompleteness of the schools record and indicated his intent to move toward greater efficiency. In a Supplementary Report, Jessop also asserted even in those early days the Province's emerging need for post-secondary education capability, suggesting:

*The fact, too, that British Columbia will soon require a
Provincial University capable of conferring degrees in arts,
law, and medicine, should not be lost sight of; and public
lands in aid of such an institution should be granted at the
outset of our career, as an integral portion of the Dominion of
Canada.[21]*

Those were prophetic words that marked a lengthy skirmish
between Victoria and Vancouver over where the province's
university should be located. The debate would assume a life of its
own over the next 40 or more years, ending its initial phase with
the establishment of the University of British Columbia at
Vancouver's Point Grey. For the moment, though, Jessop's primary
concern was with assembling a system of public schooling.

Struggling to Staff the Schools

The efforts of John Jessop, British Columbia's first
Superintendent of Education under the new legislation, to create
an orderly school system would require much more time than
would be available to him. Jessop's tenure lasted only about five
years after the introduction of the first Act. This was a scattered,
sparsely populated province with very few schools, a frontier
mentality, little consistency around what constituted acceptable
teaching, and even in the early days, some thorny issues around
teacher compensation. Even the matter of locating
accommodation for teachers in small rural communities was
problematic: "In nearly all our outlying school districts teachers
find great difficulty in obtaining board and lodging. Farm-houses,
in some cases, are too far from the school, and in others devoid of
accommodation for any one outside the family."[22]

Jessop captured several of the day's issues in a section of his
1872-73 report headed "Inadequacy of Teachers' Salaries." The
text of the report was curiously two-handed – at once both
demeaning to and complimentary regarding female teachers. His
urging that Trustees hire "efficient female teachers" was clear
encouragement for his effort to save money by hiring the best for
less:

*The evils of so-called cheap, and necessarily inefficient
teaching, cannot be overestimated. Although our country*

schools are small, yet the time of each one of the pupils is as valuable as that of a pupil in the most efficient of our city schools. The pupils in our country schools being so few the salaries can scarcely be made more than the above-mentioned figure. This will have a tendency to throw many of them into the hands of female teachers, as salaries of $60 per month would be fair remuneration for them. It is a generally conceded fact that female teachers, as a rule, possess greater aptitude for communicating knowledge, and are usually better disciplinarians, especially among young children, than males. Woman's mission is pre-eminently that of an educator. Her softening, refining, and elevating influence contributes largely to success in the school-room. Patient and painstaking, she rules through the affections; her authority being thus based upon love, this trait of character is thus reciprocated by those with whom she comes in contact...I feel no hesitancy in stating, therefore, that Trustees would advance the best interests of the rising generation by securing the services of efficient female teachers whenever and wherever they can be obtained.[23]

It is tempting to look with a critical 21st century gaze at the attitudes of that earlier day. Clearly there was confusion in the minds of those responsible to staff the schools. While women were considered to be naturally gifted teachers, British Columbia was seen by most as a man's province. It was located on the far western edge of the country's growth, the work and the living were rough, and though there was a place for women such as Jessop described, his concern for adequate salaries was clearly focused on securing the services of male teachers:

We can hardly expect efficient male teachers to remain in the profession permanently at $50 per month amid temptations to engage in mining, merchandise, farming, stock-raising, and before long, it is to be hoped, numerous other occupations in connection with railroad construction.[24]

Salaries remained a topic of discussion through the early years. Clearly, teachers were not viewed as professionals of the order of, say, doctors or lawyers. They tended instead to be compared to tradespeople; discussions regarding their salary situation inevitably pointed out the perceived benefits of life as a teacher:

> *While admitting the fact that salaries of Public School teachers
> are lower in this Province than they ought to be, and that they
> compare unfavourably with the wages of artisans and skilled
> labourers, yet when we take into consideration the many
> advantages that teachers have over the other class in the
> items of sure pay all the year round, light work in a large
> majority of the districts, short hours, and consequently many
> opportunities for mental improvement, they certainly, in this
> respect, have but little to complain of.[25]*

It appears little has changed over the years in regard to some
elements of the popular mythology surrounding teaching. Teachers
have long responded to the charges leveled in the Annual Report
of 1875; that their work is less than demanding, that their hours
are short, and that they enjoy the comfort of assured employment
and guaranteed income. This was official comment in one of the
few documents on record from those early days of public
education in British Columbia. The message might well have been
intended for the legislators of the day; it demonstrated little
awareness or appreciation of the reality of life for teachers at
work. Their schools were often crude, frequently undersupported
and undersupplied. The majority of them were located, to use the
popular British Columbia term, in areas "beyond Hope."

Quickly, a soon-to-become perennial theme emerged. Despite
the shortcomings that might have been perceived by its teachers,
British Columbia was depicted in the Annual Report of 1873-74 as
possessing great benefits. Although its opening comment
expressed concern about the Province's lack of teachers with
professional training, its concluding note under the heading
"Scarcity of trained teachers" suggested, perhaps optimistically,
that the natural advantages of British Columbia should more than
overcome the difficulty:

> *Want of properly trained teachers is a great drawback to the
> efficiency of the Public Schools in the Province. Among the
> thirty-six teachers in the employ of the Department during the
> past year, only eight have undergone regular training for the
> profession . . . At the present time there are more schools
> under unqualified teachers than at the date of my last Report .
> . . This state of things will continue until a stronger tide of
> immigration sets in, or till we can educate and train them for
> the work here, or offer such salaries as will induce professional*

teachers to settle in the Province . . . While our salaries are lower than could be wished, yet they compare very favourably with what teachers obtain elsewhere; and should, one would think, when taken in connection with the numerous advantages enjoyed here with regard to climate and natural resources, secure for us an ample supply of good teachers.[26]

Despite his apparent confidence, Jessop realized that the Province had an insufficient supply of teachers and that the problem was unlikely to disappear until a "made in British Columbia" teacher training capability was developed. He sought help from colleagues elsewhere in Canada. In a letter to Dr. James Carlyle, Second Master at Toronto Normal School, Jessop outlined the Province's problem:

We have been labouring under serious disadvantages so far for want of a supply of qualified teachers, and, in the absence of a Normal School, which, however, will be established as soon as practicable, we must keep up our teaching staff by importations.[27]

Clearly, despite his expressed confidence that teachers would be drawn to the schools of British Columbia, Jessop had misgivings. In an effort to broaden his outreach to Eastern markets, he wrote a letter to the Editor of the Toronto Globe:

the great difficulty in obtaining Public School teachers under which we have been labouring almost from the commencement of our present system of education, obliged us to put forth vigorous efforts to induce young and promising pupils to enter the profession. These efforts are likely to prove successful, so that hereafter British Columbia, to a great extent at least, will be in a position to supply her own teachers.[28]

It would be some years before British Columbia would address the challenge of establishing at-home programs of teacher preparation. The problem of supplying a sufficient number of teachers for Canada's westernmost province would not soon be resolved. For many years the Province would have to reply on its ability to attract teachers from elsewhere, a reality cited in the 1873 Annual Report under the heading "Want of Uniformity in Teaching:"

In the absence of a Training School, the great diversity in methods of teaching in British Columbia is not to be wondered at; especially when we consider that the teachers hail from England, Ireland, and Scotland, Ontario, Quebec, and New Brunswick, Australia, New Zealand, and the United States.[29]

John Jessop continued to face the problem of a teacher shortage throughout his tenure as Superintendent. He was clear about the seriousness of the problem, noting the challenge it posed for the Board of Education:

> *The great want, the most serious drawback in the successful progress of our school system, has been, and is, the total inadequacy of the supply of competent teachers for the demands of the Province; and while this obstacle remains in the way it will be impracticable for the Board of Education to carry out in their entirety the rules and regulations pertaining to teachers' salaries.*[30]

Ten or more years after John Jessop's departure from the scene, there was evidence that much work remained, at least insofar as some local school officials were concerned. Reports from inspectors and correspondence to the Superintendent were opportunities to plead one's case or to vent frustrations. Clearly, teachers' work in British Columbia was still in its infancy, marked in many cases by different and indifferent expectations regarding proper practice. The problem was particularly acute in the small rural communities, where for good or for bad, the previous teacher had always left a mark. In one recorded instance, the expressed concerns were basic, as noted in a secretary's letter to a school board:

> *Before we got our present teacher we were never troubled about the lighting of the fires, sweeping, etc . . . but our present teacher will not do it. She says it is no part of her duties. The children very precociously say that they come to school to learn, and not to soil their clothes with work . . . But it is the way, the less people have to do, the less they want to do.*[31]

Initial Support and a New Regime

Interestingly, and perhaps typical of prevailing views, Superintendent of Education John Jessop, though presumably himself a certificated teacher as required by Bill 16, made no mention in his 1872 report of teacher education as a part of a proposed university for British Columbia. Perhaps he considered the preparation of teachers to be of a different order than was a university education. Certainly, there seemed to be considerable doubt in the public mind that preparation to teach was a post-secondary education activity. Rather, it was identified as a *training* need. In his 1873 report, Jessop commented on the current state of affairs in the classrooms of the Province, observing that:

> *A Training School will soon become a necessity in this Province; but until such an institution can be established something might be accomplished in securing uniformity of method by inaugurating Teachers' Conventions, or Institutes where time-tables and programmes of study could be submitted and different methods of teaching discussed, with a view to adopting some regular system in all schools that may be about equal in attendance and requirements.[32]*

The Superintendent moved ahead quickly with his plan to establish a Teachers' Convention, which he would chair and which he saw as having the potential to bring order to classroom practice. In 1874, Jessop proposed:

> *to hold the first meeting of the institute July next, during the time of the annual teachers' examination, when lectures and addresses will be delivered, papers read, and discussions held on various subjects connected with education and the different methods of teaching . . . Among the first beneficial results which I anticipate from the establishment of this convention is the attainment of more uniformity in the methods of teaching.[33]*

Jessop was obviously pleased with the outcome of the first Teachers' Convention. In his report following the inaugural 1875 session he observed:

> *Although imperfectly organized as yet, on account of its being a new thing in this Province, and the great difficulty of getting its scattered members together for consultation and routine work, yet the movement has taken sufficient root to warrant the assertion that the teachers would not willingly allow it to be discontinued . . . from 20 to 25 teachers, among others, took part in the proceedings.[34]*

Relatively quickly, participants in the Teachers' Convention began to advance the idea that experience would be more important than further training in determining tenure as a teacher. There was little consistency in personnel practice around the province, and that situation would persist for some years. On the matter of certification, though, which was a provincial responsibility, the participants in the 1876-77 Convention spoke clearly:

> *It was proposed that all teachers be required to teach for two years as third-class teachers; on showing aptitude to teach they be allowed to undergo examination as second-class teachers, which position they may hold for two years, then be eligible to pass necessary examination as first-class teachers. Rule to apply to all teachers except those holding first-class certificates from the older Provinces of the Dominion or graduated of a British university; that they be eligible for examination as first-class teachers if they have taught four years. The principal object to be gained is aptitude to teach; success as an instructor and experience would then be valued which at present is not. It was insisted on by some teachers that when they once obtain a first grade A certificate, it should be for life, as in other professions. Matter left over until next year.*[35]

The final sentence may have been significant. Certainly Jessop, as Superintendent of Education and President of the Teachers' Convention, was the individual primarily responsible for the certification of teachers. Perhaps he was personally more persuaded of the importance of further training than of certificates for life. However, change was in the wind – Jessop's departure was imminent.

The report for the 1877-78 school year was filed by a new Superintendent of Education, C. C. McKenzie, who pointedly distanced himself from all events preceding his tenure. McKenzie entered his report on the Teachers' Convention of 1878 entirely within quotation marks and attributed its content to Mr. Halliday, the honourary secretary. The substance of the Convention was noted briefly: the teacher examination papers, Mr. Jessop's report on a trip he had taken, and three papers delivered by attendees. Other excerpts from Mr. Halliday's report were tantalizing in their shortage of detail: "Mr. Jessop opened the proceedings by foreshadowing certain reported changes in the school system...was presented with an address. The Government was petitioned not to make any changes in the Superintendency."[36] Those discussions about changes in the Act and in the Superintendency are matters for consideration elsewhere, but the incoming McKenzie asserted clearly that prior operations were none of his responsibility:

> *As the scholastic year terminated prior to my appointment I am not in a position to make further comment on its operations, nor do I feel authorized to go into the history of events that have taken place and which properly belong to the next year.[37]*

The "certain reported changes" that John Jessop had previously noted included the passing of a new School Act and Regulations, and replacement of the Province's Board of Education with a system of local school boards. In his first report, Superintendent McKenzie was quick to point a finger regarding its troublesome lateness and the incompleteness of the record:

> *The non-transmission by the late Deputy Superintendent of Education of his notes of inspection of schools and by the Trustees of important schools of their annual school reports, coupled with the shortness of the time since my appointment, has delayed the issue of this Report till this date . . . I am compelled to hand in this Report in its present incomplete state, and to defer to a Supplementary Report the rest of the special reports on District Schools.[38]*

This changing of the guard and the introduction of new schools legislation may have signalled much broader concerns with the state of the Province's fledgling school system. The new Act abandoned the idea of a single Board of Education in favour of a system of local boards of school trustees. In McKenzie's view, the former regime represented a school system in chaos, a system populated by rebellious teachers. He reported at considerable length on what he saw as the shortcomings of the schools and particularly their teachers:

> *The voluntary resignation of the Board of Education and their Chairman led to my appointment as Superintendent of Education on the 9th September, 1878, and I have thus held the position for the space of one year. I have striven during that*

time to promote in every possible way the best educational interests of the Province and have endeavoured to carry out the spirit and letter of the School Act. Every attempt to alter or improve the previously existing state of things has, however, met with strenuous and determined opposition from some quarter or other, and not less from teachers than from others. Under the former regime, these as a body were allowed the utmost freedom and latitude in the internal and external management of their schools, and the quotation "Every man did that which was right in his own eyes" not inaptly describes the state of affairs as it then existed and so far as that concerned them. They chose their own time for opening their schools, absented themselves when they pleased and on trivial grounds, and closed their schools early or late as it suited their convenience; children went to school from the beginning to the end of the year, and in most cases, except perhaps the teacher, no one, whether parent, trustee, superintendent, or board knew what progress was being made or what was the actual condition of things. The annual reports of trustees in the parts filled in by teachers were full of inaccuracies. Teachers to this day manifest the utmost reluctance to make corrections to these reports, and in some cases evince a sublime indifference as to whether they are made out at all. On the whole I cannot forbear from saying that the utmost carelessness and indifference exist among teachers as to whether the statistical and other information they supply is at all accurate, and if their zeal educationally is to be gauged by the amount of it they display in their communication with the Education Office, the Province has need to demand of its servants thorough reformation in both.

My first care as Superintendent of Education was the preparation of the School Report of 1877-78. Instead of falling still-born from the press, like previous reports, the issue of that document was the signal for a series of violent attacks. Its grammar was criticized, its facts were disputed, and its suggestions were weighed in the balances and found wanting. No necessity exists for defence of the Report on any of those points, but, before dismissing this question, I must here reiterate the assertion in the Report on which the attack was principally grounded, that certificates had not been altogether

*impartially granted by the late Board of Education, and say in
addition that the revocation of these certificates is
imperatively called for.[39]*

In Search of a Better Way

For several years following 1878, there was no mention of the
Teachers' Convention in the Annual Reports on the public school
system. That may have reflected the decentralization that
occurred with the creation of local school boards. The tone of
Superintendent McKenzie's remarks did not appear likely to
encourage the development of warm relations between British
Columbia's teachers and the Department of Education over the
coming years. However, the effort continued, though its reporting
was sparse and there may have been breaks in the continuity of
the program. The Annual Report of 1889 referred to the
postponement of that year's events and to a preceding four-period
that might have indicated another hiatus:

> *It is to be regretted that the Executive of the Provincial
> Teachers' Institute deemed it advisable to postpone the annual
> meeting in 1889. The convocations held thus far have been of
> great benefit to those who have not had the advantage of a
> Normal School training, as well as having been entertaining
> and instructive to teachers who have spent years in the
> profession. In fact, everyone who, with a view to self-
> improvement, attended the meetings held during the past four
> years will, undoubtedly, concur in the statement that these
> convocations were productive of much practical benefit.[40]*

The continuing education of teachers through summer courses
eventually became a regular part of the culture of public school
education in British Columbia. The Summer School Supervisor's
report on the sessions of 1914 and 1915 noted that

> *the object of these courses was to increase the efficiency of the
> Provincial schools by giving teachers the opportunity to
> strengthen their grasp of certain subjects, and to qualify
> themselves further along certain special lines of school-work.[41]*

Summer school was a sponsored activity: "Teachers who were
admitted to these courses received free tuition, transportation, and
a per diem allowance of $1 toward living expenses provided the
attendance was regular and the work satisfactory."[42] The 1914

session offered courses in Rural Science and School-gardening, Manual Training, Manual Arts, Household Economics, Art, and Music to a total of 513 teachers. In 1915, English Literature and French were added and total enrolment increased to 690 teachers. According to the official record, the activity was a success:

> *Victoria proved itself to be an ideal location for a summer school, and the work in both years was not handicapped by any extreme weather conditions. A large amount of outdoor study was carried on, and it was the aim of the staff to make the work as pleasant as possible. Social gatherings were held frequently, where opportunity was given to the teachers to meet and become acquainted. The good-fellowship promoted by these gatherings and the opportunity afforded by the summer classes for an exchange of ideas and a discussion of school problems in itself could not fail to be very beneficial, and the majority of the students must have returned to their schools with increased zeal and a wider outlook.[43]*

The teachers who attended summer school were not totally occupied with the solitary pursuit of their studies. In various ways, they formed a community, even though they were together for only a few weeks before returning to their own towns and villages. Their charitable endeavours one year reflected awareness of the cataclysmic events taking place far away but affecting their friends and relatives – World War I:

> *During the session of 1915 the sum of $1,000 was contributed by the staff and students for the purchase of a machine gun for the 47th Battalion, C.E.F., of which the Commanding Officer is Lieutenant-Colonel Winsby, Inspector of Schools. Further contributions were made to the Canadian Red Cross and the French Red Cross Societies.[44]*

For more than 25 years before 1901, a set of qualifying examinations had been the sole test of the capability of a prospective teacher in British Columbia. The topics, questions and examiners changed over the years, and that information was routinely published the following year in the Annual Report, along with the names of the successful candidates.

There was from almost the beginning of the province's history, a call for a set of more systematic teacher certification protocols. That would not occur until the 1901 establishment of the Vancouver Provincial Normal School. Prior to that, British

Columbia relied on candidates passing examinations of their choosing, and in some cases on their having completed a training program in another jurisdiction. Nevertheless, the work continued. In 1873, recognizing the challenge of identifying teachers for rural schools, the Department made a less-than-successful effort at least to decentralize the teacher examination process:

> *For the accommodation of teachers, and others wishing to become such, residing in the interior, an examination was held at Clinton . . . Only two candidates, however, took the work, one of whom failed.*[45]

In the early years, prospective British Columbia public school teachers were simply required to complete public (elementary) school themselves before presenting as candidates for certification. That reality was acknowledged in the ninth Annual Report under the heading "Regulations For Admission, &c., Into High School," which stated: "Teachers of the Public Schools, who have already obtained certificates as teachers, may be permitted to enter the High School as pupils without being required to pass the usual entrance examination."[46] The policy acknowledged an existing regularity reflected in the report of the 1877 teacher examination candidate group that: "several of them however were pupils from the High School, too young to receive appointments as teachers, but nearly all succeeded in obtaining certificates."[47]

Previously I noted an 1878 comment of newly appointed Superintendent of Education C.C. McKenzie regarding a perception of unfairness in the certification process. That comment may perhaps have originated from a practice described in the 1877 Annual Report that in later years might have been either applauded or decried as an example of affirmative action. That practice had reinforced a somewhat peculiar stance of the Department of Education, according to comments in various Annual Reports, regarding female teachers. The 1878 Report noted a concern regarding the practices surrounding teacher examinations and the corrective action taken by the Board of Education:

> *At this and all preceding examinations two standards of marks were used; one consisting of the aggregate number for all the subjects for male candidates, while for females the value placed upon euclid, mensuration, algebra and book-keeping was dropped, and the total of the remaining subjects used as a*

divisor in estimating the percentage of answering. This system has been looked upon as giving the ladies an undue advantage over the other sex, and from time to time complaints have been made respecting it. At a recent meeting of the Board of Education the question was fully discussed and the conclusion arrived at, that in future no difference should be made; lady applicants must therefore govern themselves accordingly. Placing all on an equality in this respect will of course enhance the value of certificates obtained hereafter by ladies; as in order to secure a first-class certificate most, if not all, the mathematical subjects will have to be taken, and a fair percentage of marks required for them.[48]

Every substantive decision made regarding a publicly regarded and regulated activity contributes to development of public perceptions of that activity and its practitioners. This minimal requirement for the educational background and preparation of candidates for teaching certificates probably reflected a problem of supply and demand – British Columbia had no readily available pool of professionally trained teachers. That limited requirement probably contributed also to the early and persistent identification of teaching and teacher preparation as activities more appropriately associated with the trades and skilled labouring occupations than with higher education. The theme recurred many years later, when the University of British Columbia Senate turned down a request to recognize Normal School courses for post-secondary credit.

To date, in addition to John Jessop's early public and private appeals to the Ontario teacher market, the Department had continued to point out the need for programs of teacher preparation. However, officials had taken no action. In fact, in 1878 Superintendent C.C. McKenzie opined that "so far at least as education is concerned, this Province is able to educate its own teachers, provided advantage is taken of the means ready to that end."[49] He was commenting in reference to the third-place candidate among the current year's examinees, a locally-schooled man described as performing very well, even in comparison to others with experience and those from other provinces. His reference to "the means ready" was vague and he offered no further comment. Perhaps McKenzie was underlining his non-association with what had occurred previously, including the call for a normal school.

McKenzie continued to mount what appeared to be a campaign to raise the public standing of British Columbia's teachers and to improve their conditions of work. In reality, his effort could also be described as a defence of the status quo in regard to teacher certification and the educational process leading up to it. He noted that 6 of the 58 teachers then employed by the Department had attended British Columbia schools, and suggested that "should sufficient inducements be held out, more would in all probability follow their example."[50]

These locally educated teachers were viewed by some, perhaps including their formally trained colleagues from elsewhere and some cost-conscious school authorities, as less than fully qualified. In this case, whatever his motivations, McKenzie professed support for these teachers, who he described as being unjustly and prejudicially treated. In his view, they deserved better:

> Hitherto, the prejudice contained in the old proverb, "no prophet is without honour save in his own country" seems to have operated against them with the educational authorities. They have had the misnomer of "pupil teachers" and although in most cases holding certificates have been paid at the rate of half the salary usually paid to an uncertificated teacher. It will also be found in every instance that these so-called pupil teachers have been successful in their schools or classes, and that increased attendance and progress has been the result of their labours, so that it may safely be said of our teachers of home-growth that they are "not a whit behind the very chiefest apostles" whom we have imported or who have come to our country on their own responsibility. The injustice of paying a salary of $20 per month to a teacher with a class of 70, 80 or 90 scholars is too evident to need comment, and not only is there no money equivalent for the work done but the very fact of teaching in the lowest division of a school (the place assigned to pupil teachers) prevents, or does not help, that self-improvement in the knowledge necessary for the acquirement of a higher certificate.[51]

Eventually, McKenzie would add his voice to those of other officials calling for the establishment of a normal school in the Province. However, even his 1881 comment was couched within a positive affirmation of current practice and an observation that suggested an in-Province teacher-training institution was a project for a future occasion. In a curious twist of logic, McKenzie asserted that British Columbia's locally high-schooled teachers were likely better at their jobs than were normal school-trained immigrants from other provinces, even as he pointed out the need for a normal school in British Columbia:

The number of candidates for certificates from persons educated in this Province is steadily increasing. Those who presented themselves for examination for the first time at the late examination formed a great part of the number examined, and were largely made up of young persons trained at the Victoria High School. This highly useful institution has now supplied our public schools with so many teachers that nearly half of the certificated teachers have been educated in the Province. These teachers, I am happy to say, have all the necessary qualifications in the matter of education, and in other respects also compare very favourably with the rest of our teachers. Having youth, they have the enthusiasm of beginners, and are in all probability better capable of doing the work for which they are destined than would be those normally trained teachers whom we could attract to our schools from the other Provinces of the Dominion. But, though the good education given compensates in part for the want of professional training, the Province will still continue to feel the want of a Normal School until its resources and population justify the opening of such an institution. At present the High School supplies, as far as it can, this desideratum, and it has well and worthily done so.[52]

The tone of McKenzie's remarks was echoed somewhat in his successor S.D. Pope's report on the Public School Teachers' Examination of 1889. Pope had clear and definite views on what was necessary to be an effective teacher. His remarks carried the idea that there was more to teaching than scholarship, suggesting in an early day the sometimes defensive stance of a West asserting that it was as good as, if not better than, the distant East (perhaps referring to Ontario). Pope challenged the notion that higher certification was in itself an indicator of better practice:

While these certificates are merely assurances of educational standing and by no means imply ability to impart instruction, yet the higher the certificate held, or in other words the greater the amount of knowledge possessed by the teacher, the greater the confidence to be placed in him as an instructor, and the more apt he is to become successful in his profession; still a man may possess an excellent education and be wanting in capability as an instructor. There is a difference between a scholar *and a* teacher. *The advanced intelligence of the day demands of the instructor more than* book-learning.

The teacher may rank high at his qualifying examination, but if he does not possess culture *he is not thoroughly equipped for his work. As the mind of a child receives lasting impressions from surrounding influences and is to a high degree imitative, the teacher's manner and actions should have a refining influence on the character of the child, and should impart a love for virtue and morality.*

The teacher who possesses culture is immeasurably to be preferred to one devoid of it. There is no room in the profession for him who does not combine the gentleman *with the* scholar.

That all of our schools are yearly taking a higher standard in advanced work, as well as the fact that the supply of teachers at the present time nearly equals the demand, renders it thoroughly necessary that those who are admitted to the profession be prepared to give instruction in the subjects which they will be required to teach.[53]

The final paragraph of Pope's comment carried, albeit indirectly, the notion that teacher preparation was important. By 1892, he too was urging the establishment of a normal school:

The need of a Normal School has been very generally recognized for a considerable time. The chief benefits arising from such an institution lie in the good work it accomplishes for the public schools in producing for them teachers properly trained for their work, and possessed of a knowledge of those methods of imparting instruction which are essential to success in the school-room...We cannot too strongly urge the early establishment of such an institution in the Province.[54]

Even before the days of British Columbia's normal schools, and certainly during their existence, there was a strong emphasis on the management side of schooling. Many comments in Inspectors' reports focused on the evident and apparent, such as records and the submission of reports. The Annual Report of 1893, perhaps with a tone of discouragement or at least frustration, indirectly referred to the shortcomings of a system of preparation that obtained the service of teachers before it was assured of their maturity:

> *The young woman of sixteen or eighteen, and the young man of eighteen or twenty, who obtain certificates of qualification to teach and yet scarcely know the difference between a register and a recitation record-book, or who cannot make out correctly the monthly and yearly reports required, are certainly not prepared for the profession. It is eminently necessary for the teacher to have a good educational standing, but it is equally important that he have a good knowledge of everything required for the proper management of a school.[55]*

Throughout many early comments on the state of schooling in British Columbia, there was a clear lack of consensus on just what constituted good teaching. Some observations appeared simply to reflect the biases of the individual observer, uninformed by any systematic body of knowledge or theory of teaching. It was clear, though, that there was a distinction between academic education, which might evidence scholarship rather than aptitude, and preparation for teaching, which in 1895 called for the development of the well-rounded person:

> *After obtaining a certificate the inexperienced teacher must, in order to succeed, acquire a good knowledge of the best methods now used in schools, must study how to apply them to advantage, and must make himself familiar with the school system under which he is to teach. In fact, the teacher in order to become successful in the profession must be a diligent student.*
>
> *A few years past the idea seemed to be a prevalent one, that any person who held a certificate could teach school. This was a very erroneous conclusion. As well might we say that every man who has studied the art of navigation could be entrusted with a ship at sea, or that every woman who has studied painting for a limited time could produce a masterpiece, as to advance the idea that book learning is all that is required for the teacher's profession. Teaching power, aptness, and skill are additional qualifications indispensable to success. Aptitude to teach is a result of skill and tact, combined with a thorough*

knowledge of the means of obtaining good order and discipline and of properly managing the work of the schoolroom. To these must be added as essential to the instructor, the possession of a high moral character and refined manners.[56]

In the minds of many the preparation of capable teachers was the work of a normal school, but such an institution did not yet exist in British Columbia. The sparse written record that characterizes much of the early story of teacher education in this province offers little evidence of any broader discussion that may have been taking place prior to 1900. The call, however, was repeated often. D. Wilson, an Inspector of Schools, was critical of the situation in elementary schools. In his 1895 report to Superintendent Pope, Wilson supported the Superintendent's call for systematic teacher preparation:

In methods of primary instruction our schools, with some exceptions, are certainly inferior. This defect I can only ascribe to the absence of a Normal School, where suitable professional training could be given to those who propose to take up the difficult work of teaching. The establishment of such an institution has, on more than one occasion, been strongly advocated by you in the Annual School Report, and I trust that the time is not far distant when your valuable recommendation will be carried out.[57]

Not content to wait for action from the provincial government, the Board of School Trustees of the City of Victoria in 1895 developed their own innovative plan to meet the need for teachers in that district. In effect, their plan was a local version of certification, albeit for substitute teaching, with all of the documentary trappings of a regularly-issued certificate:

With a view to the best interests of education in this city, and there not as yet being a Provincial Normal School at which young teachers could receive training in the best methods of educating, the Board by resolution decided in April to appoint a pupil-teacher to each of the graded schools. No salary is attached to the position thus created, but the appointees have the prior right of engagement as substitutes. By subsequent resolution those pupil-teachers who had served for six months in that capacity can undergo an examination conducted by the Principals of the Graded Schools, as an Examining Board, in the practical work of teaching. Upon the result of this examination, as certified by the Examining Board, a certificate is issued by the Board of Trustees under seal, and signed by the Examining Board and Secretary and Chairman of the School Board. Judging by the number of applications received for the position of pupil-teacher in our schools this movement has been an unqualified success.[58]

Superintendent of Education Pope continued his efforts to convince the Province to establish a Normal School. His 1895 report included a section headed 'Normal School,' perhaps with the hope that action might finally taken toward addressing the challenges of teacher supply and demand. Pope's tone was urgent:

We again beg to recommend that immediate steps be taken towards the establishment of a Normal School in this Province. It is of paramount importance that the young and inexperienced aspirants for the position of teachers have some special preparation for their work. The success of the school is wholly dependent on the capability and fitness of the teacher, and the vital interests of children should not be entrusted to one who is ignorant of the first principles of the art of teaching ... A Normal School affords to teachers the opportunity of properly preparing themselves for the achievement of the best results. While it is true that every teacher who has attended a Normal School may not prove to be a successful instructor, yet we believe that he will accomplish much more from the training he received in such an institution. It is also true that some of our best teachers have never attended a Normal School, but their success must be attributed either to natural aptitude, or to many years of experience, or to both combined... It is proper to add, that British Columbia is the only Province of the Dominion, which does not support one or more Normal Schools.[59]

Perhaps at last Pope had begun to gain the attention of government. It would be another five years, though, before British Columbia's first institution for the preparation of teachers, the Vancouver Provincial Normal School, would commence operation. A movement that began in France in the first half of the 19th century and subsequently took root in North America, first in the United States and subsequently in Canada, would finally reach the West.

Notes to Chapter 1

1 Frank Peake, *The Anglican Church in British Columbia* (Vancouver, BC: Mitchell Press, 1959), 7.
2 Province of British Columbia. *An Act Respecting Public Schools* (Victoria, 1872). [Hereafter *PSA 1872*]. Note to reader: This legislation is printed in ARPS 1872, cited below. Page numbers are ARPS pages.
3 Province of British Columbia. *First Annual Report on the Public Schools in the Province of British Columbia*, [Hereafter these annual reports are referred to by year as *ARPS*], (Victoria: Government Printer, 1872).
4 *PSA 1872*, Section 4, 11.
5 Ibid.
6 Ibid., Section 7 (6), 12.
7 Ibid., Appendix C, 21.
8 Ibid.
9 *ARPS 1872*, 21.
10 Ibid.
11 Ibid, 28-30.
12 Ibid, 30.
13 *PSA 1872, Appendix B*, 19.
14 Ibid.
15 Ibid.
16 Charles Dickens, *Barnaby Rudge: A Tale of the Riots of Eighty* (London: Odhams), 116.
17 *ARPS 1874*, 26.
18 *ARPS 1875*, 27.
19 *ARPS 1872*, 30.
20 Ibid, 31.
21 *ARPS 1872, Supplementary Report*, 44.
22 *ARPS 1873*, 8.
23 Ibid., 7.
24 *ARPS 1875*, 9.
25 Ibid., 7.
26 *ARPS 1874*, 22.
27 John Jessop to Dr. James Carlyle, Second Master, Toronto Normal School, April 12, 1875, cited in ARPS 1875, 13.
28 *ARPS 1877*, 67.
29 *ARPS 1873*, 7.
30 *ARPS 1875*, 8.
31 *ARPS 1889*, 261.
32 *ARPS 1873*, 8.
33 *ARPS 1874*, 23, 24.
34 *ARPS 1875*, 17.
35 *ARPS 1877*, 10-11.
36 *ARPS 1878*, 181.
37 Ibid.
38 *ARPS 1879*, 179, 185.
39 Ibid., 161-162.
40 *ARPS 1889*, p. 261.
41 *ARPS 1915*, p. 56.
42 Ibid., p. 56.
43 Ibid., p. 64.
44 *ARPS 1915*, p. 64.
45 Ibid, 10.
46 *ARPS 1880*, 359.
47 *ARPS 1877*, 10.
48 *ARPS 1874*, 26.
49 *ARPS 1878*, 180.
50 Ibid.
51 Ibid.
52 *ARPS 1881*, 253.
53 *ARPS 1889*, 203.
54 *ARPS 1892*, 253.
55 *ARPS 1893*, 8.
56 *ARPS 1895*, 209.
57 Ibid, 213.
58 Ibid, 224.
59 *ARPS 1896*, 290-291.

LEARNING TO TEACH

TEACHER PREPARATION
IN VICTORIA, BC
1903-1963

Chapter 2
The Normal Life:
Establishing Teacher Training

While I was writing this book, I was often asked the question, "What does the term *normal school* mean?" The term *école normale*, borrowed from the French to describe the training of (primarily) elementary school teachers can be somewhat misleading when translated into English. We tend to think of *normal* as meaning ordinary, usual, and without surprises. The Merriam-Webster Dictionary defines *normal* as "according with, constituting, or not deviating from a norm, rule, or principle; and conforming to a type, standard, or regular pattern." In English, we have defined the root word, *norm*, as an authoritative standard, and a principle of right action binding upon the members of a group and serving to guide, control, or regulate proper and acceptable behaviour.

In French, the term refers to a normative operation, a standard by which practice can be judged. We might have preferred the term *model school* to describe these institutions, but that descriptor was used later to describe the classes of elementary school pupils placed within British Columbia's normal schools. Those seats were highly sought after by parents seeking a quality elementary education for their children, because the classes were seen to have been carefully staffed with 'model' teachers. Like the unique British use of the term *public school*, which in Canada refers to a private school, the term *normal school* carries little meaning for any except those who were its students or who have studied the history of the normal school movement.

North American normal schools came into being at least partly as a result of settlement, urbanization, and an unprecedented need for public school teachers. It was generally assumed that teaching was an occupation requiring little professional knowledge or skill. Certainly it was not considered to be an academic occupation. For the most part, the public was apathetic toward normal schools and the attitude of the universities towards teacher preparation was dismissive. As a result, the normal schools were established outside the realm of the universities, and the gulf between their intellectual and philosophical foundations and those of the academy persisted for many years.[1] Despite that, the normal school movement in North America represented a significant and influential stage in the development of teacher education. In British Columbia, a half-century of normal school training ended in 1956 as the first significant step was taken to move the practice and the study of teacher education into the university system.

Roots of the Normal School Movement

Several developments in North American life in the nineteenth century contributed to the introduction of normal schools. There was a marked and rapid increase in the population of the continent. The impact of the industrial revolution was being felt in all quarters, and Canada and the United States were urbanizing rapidly. The political climate that promoted democracy as a system of government also paved the way for free education within a public school system. The progress of professionalism in medicine and science encouraged society to pay greater attention to the needs of schools and to demand well-trained teachers. The concept of public education imported from Europe increased society's awareness of the need for organized teacher-preparation centers.[2] The Normal Schools were particularly concerned with fundamentals, principles, rules, and methods that would provide teachers with a model to direct their practice roles. From their inception they were separated not only from the university but also in many cases from the secondary school system and the preparation of secondary school teachers.[3]

During the second quarter of the nineteenth century, educators such as Horace Mann and Edgerton Ryerson were impressed by the programs that they had seen in Europe, including the École

Normale Superieure in Paris and the teachers' seminaries of Prussia.[4] However, many other proponents of formalized teacher training knew nothing about these European institutions, and most knew little of the origin of the idea.

In the period between 1789 and 1860, North American communities laid the foundations of the public school system and established the first normal schools to meet the growing demand for trained teachers.[5] The movement faced opposition on the basis of two somewhat contradictory lines of attack. First, the critics asserted that anyone who knew a subject could teach it. Second, they insisted that normal schools should offer only methods and education courses. In America this characterized much of the debate from 1850 to 1870.[6] However, the success of the normal school movement was due to the sound logic inherent in its priorities; that teachers needed specific training in institutions devoted to that end, that graduates of these schools were better teachers than those educated elsewhere, and that there was pressing demand for teachers to staff the newly created public schools.[7]

Initially, a typical minimum course was one year in duration and included six basic categories: (1) common subject areas, (2) academic subjects covered in the school curriculum, (3) physical, mental, and moral childhood development, (4) principles and methods of teaching, (5) school government, and (6) practice teaching.[8] But by 1900 some normal schools in America were offering a general degree course of two years, a specialized degree course of two years, a general diploma course of four years, a specialized four-year course, and a course of one year for college graduates.[9] Recruits were to possess: (1) moral and religious character, (2) good health, (3) good manners, (4) love of children, (5) adequate amounts of talent and information, (6) tact for teaching and governing others, (7) love for occupations of the schoolroom, (8) common school and martyr spirit, and (9) some experience in teaching.[10]

The normal schools began to transform teacher training into professional preparation, an approach that received a cool reception from some colleges and universities. It did this by developing a professional attitude towards teaching, by stimulating an interest in the education of children, and by serving the needs of the public school system while improving existing classroom practices. Normal schools were an indispensable part of the system of popular education and the progress and development of all its elements.

The normal schools became a valuable agency for in-service training and initiated the concept of professionalized subject matter. They emphasized the laboratory approach to education through supervision of student teaching, attempting to duplicate or at least simulate the conditions students would encounter in the field. Further, they considered the 'extra-curriculum' activities of music and art as integral aspects of teacher preparation. But perhaps the most important aspect of the normal school's character was its pragmatic approach to meeting needs by adopting any source, material, or method that had direct bearing on facilitating public education.[11]

Horace Mann and Normal Schools in America

In the early part of the nineteenth century, some opinion suggested that individuals often became teachers because it was easier than manual labour or because they were untrained for other types of work. Pragmatically speaking, teaching could also alleviate problems caused by short periods of unemployment. James C. Carter publicized these concerns and advocated for change in the quality of teachers by calling for the establishment of teacher training institutions.[12] During the 1820s, Carter turned the attention of educational leaders to the relationship between teacher education and school improvement and proposed the establishment of a public Normal School. This institution would concentrate on subjects to be taught and on methods of teaching, with a practice school where teaching performance could be seen in action.[13] Although such an institution failed to be established at that time, Horace Mann later took up Carter's initiative and was an enthusiastic proponent of normal schools, translating his public addresses into action.[14]

More than any other individual, the inception of Normal Schools in North America can be credited to Horace Mann.[15] While other educators preceded him in their speculative emphasis on the need for teacher training, Mann was in a strategic position to implement his ideas. He ardently defended his notion that "Common Schools will never prosper without Normal Schools,"[16] declaring boldly, "I believe Normal Schools to be a new instrumentality in the advancement of the race."[17] Mann believed that with the advent of Normal Schools, he could construct an educational foundation that would serve the needs of successive generations of educators, teachers, and students: "I consider this event as marking an era in the progress of education - which, as we all know, is the progress of civilization - on this western continent and throughout the world."[18] Mann claimed confidently that "the money and the talent employed to barbarize mankind in war, if expended for education and the promotion of the arts and peace, would bring on the millennium at once."[19]

The normal schools were originally initiated in the form of two-week institutes that brought training schools to the teachers. Mann had his instructors review the fundamental rules and methods of arithmetic, grammar, writing, and basic geography. Students were continually reminded that they should "exhibit as well as explain."[20] He concluded that the art of teaching consisted of "the ability to acquire and the ability to impart, wholly different talents." In Mann's opinion, to teach effectively "includes the presentation of the different parts of a subject in a natural order, and also embraces a knowledge of methods and processes which are infinitely various."

Since educators might possess literary competence and ability to teach but lack the capability to manage a classroom, Mann's requirements for a successful teacher included management, government, and discipline of a school.[21] Mann viewed education as a broad functional process that would bring about a harmonious relation of body, intellect, and spirit. He therefore favoured a teacher-training program that would develop the individual in as many functional ways as possible.[22]

Although the need for teacher-training schools had long been recognized, Horace Mann deserves primary credit for bringing about the establishment of the first state-supported normal schools. Rather than existing as private institutions, these schools were to be owned, supported, and governed by the state for the service of public education.[23] In 1838, Mann secured $10,000 in support funding from Edmund Dwight, a prominent member of a board of education, toward the establishment of normal schools, on condition that government would match this amount.[24] A resolution was unanimously passed in the House of

Representatives and signed into law on April 19, 1838.[25]   On
July 3, 1839 the first public 'Normal School' in the United States
was opened at Lexington, Massachusetts, putting Mann's initiative
into effect.[26]   The significance of this victory was described by
Henry Barnard, an influential educational leader of the time:

> The friends of public schools, and of special institutions for the
> qualification and improvement of teachers, and of state
> supervision of the great interest of education, in every state,
> owe a large debt of gratitude to those men who achieved a
> triumph for the Board of Education, the normal schools and
> Mr. Mann, in the legislature of Massachusetts, in 1840. Defeat
> there and then . . . would have changed the whole condition of
> public instruction in this country, for half a century, if not
> forever."[27]

Edgerton Ryerson and Normal Schools in Ontario

The Canadian normal school movement spanned
approximately a century, although its history in Canada's
westernmost province was recorded during the latter half of that
period. A 1956 British Columbia Department of Education news
release announcing "Teacher training to take new trend"
commented briefly on the historical Canadian picture:

> The first government normal school in Canada was opened in
> 1836 in Montreal. This was not only the beginning of state-
> controlled teacher-training in Canada, but also on this
> continent, as the first state normal school in the United States
> did not open until 1839 at Lexington, Mass. In the half-century
> between 1847 and 1905, normal schools for training
> elementary teachers were established in every Canadian
> province. These, in most cases, were modelled after Edgerton
> Ryerson's Toronto Normal School of 1847.[28]

The Common School Act of 1846 rested on the responsibility of
government to ensure what Edgerton Ryerson recognized as the
introduction of authentic public schooling in Canada.[29] With this
system in place, Ryerson argued that the need for Normal Schools
became increasingly explicit. In his report of 1846, he made it
clear that the educational system must ensure its access to trained
teachers, a requirement that would be impossible to meet without
the formation of normal schools.[30]

However, Ryerson was not the first to appreciate the importance of teacher training. As early as 1843, Sir Francis Hincks had acknowledged that no public school system would be complete without the formation of Normal Schools.[31] Before Ryerson's appointment to superintendent of schools in 1844, no provision had been made for the practical or theoretical training of teachers.[32] There had also been no means of evaluating the qualifications of teachers, making the effectiveness of schooling in Upper Canada enormously difficult to ascertain.

Within a year of the introduction of the Common School Act, Ryerson succeeded in establishing the Toronto Normal School. With that, a standard was established for first and second class provincial certificates of teacher qualification.[33] In order to qualify for admission into the Normal School, candidates were required to meet several conditions: students must be at least sixteen years of age; they must produce a certificate of good moral character signed by a clergyman; they were required to be able to read and write; they must be acquainted with the simple rules of arithmetic, and all must declare in writing their intention to devote themselves to teaching.[34] Normal School students were expected to acquire "the habits, skills, and character structure appropriate to the morally forceful teacher." Schools operated under a strict code of behaviour that required punctuality, compliance with authority, evening curfews, and church attendance.[35]

Ryerson described his ideal for founding the Toronto Normal School of 1847 in these words: "A school in which the principles and practice of teaching according to rule are taught and exemplified".[36] He maintained that the teacher's ability to educate resided in the mental and moral power of the individual, and not merely in his technical learning.[37] Although the normal schools gave lectures on management, organization, and history of education, their strength was derived from a thorough mastery of subject areas and from supervisory criticism of the practical effectiveness of student teachers in the model school.[38] By the late 1850s normal school graduates were presented as examples and their teaching methods were used as illustrations to influence the practice of all grades of teachers.[39] Ryerson's methods helped to raise the standards of teacher education in Ontario while addressing the demand for competently trained teachers who were needed in every part of the province.[40]

Quebec's Normal Schools

The first government normal school in Canada was opened in 1836 in Montreal. This was the beginning of state-controlled teacher-training not only in Canada, but also on this continent; the first state normal school in the United States did not open until 1839 at Lexington, Massachusetts. In the half-century between 1847 and 1905, normal schools for training elementary teachers were established in every Canadian province. In most cases, they were modelled after Edgerton Ryerson's Toronto Normal School of 1847. In 1857 the McGill and Jacques Cartier Normal Schools were opened in Montreal and the Laval Normal in Quebec City, marking the beginning of systematic teacher-training in Lower Canada and the process of supplying the province with qualified teachers for its rapidly growing school system.[41] The principals who managed these schools were intensely practical and focused, with an agenda that saw the normal school as "an important lever for the elevation of English education in the province of Quebec."[42]   On March 3, 1857, the three men to whom the McGill Normal school owed its origin, Chauveau the Superintendent of Education, Bishop Fullford, and Principal Dawson, formally opened the normals. The event addressed the benefits that the province would derive from trained teachers, the sense of dedication that these teachers must possess, and the value that would be obtained from this undertaking.[43]

Qualifications for admission required that candidates must be "fully sixteen years of age and must produce a certificate of character and conduct." Additionally, each was required to "read and write sufficiently well to know the rudiments of grammar in his mother tongue, to know the Rule of Three inclusively, and to have some knowledge of geography."[44] Principal Dawson wrote to Edgerton Ryerson, then the Superintendent of Education in Ontario, and on his advice appointed Dr. Robins as Principal of the McGill Normal School. Robins was transferred from the Toronto Normal School on Ryerson's recommendation in 1857 and his position at McGill continued until 1907, when the university assumed the responsibility for training and educating teachers.[45]

Expansion to the West

Once the idea of the teacher as a trained public servant became the standard in public education, it justified a strong and positive state role in providing for teacher training through normal schools. The movement spread quickly across the continent from east to west.[46] This approach to teacher preparation became the general trend in both the United States and Canada as normal schools opened from Massachusetts (1839) to California(1875), and from Ontario (1847) and Quebec (1857) to Vancouver (1901) and Victoria (1915). Advancements in education tended to follow population patterns and the general trend of growth in urban settlements. Western normal schools had the advantage of re-examining the concept and gaining perspective on previous eastern developments in teacher training. As a result, they had consistently regulated standards and practices.

By the early 1900s normal schools had stretched to the western coast of the continent. They were by now an established institution in North America and they were considered a major agency for the preparation of teachers.[47] Western normal schools were government supported from the outset, adding further stability to the movement. They displayed a more experimental and pragmatic viewpoint than their counterparts in the East,[48] training a larger proportion of secondary teachers and maintaining overall an average of 26 percent male students.[49]

The early normal schools represented an important initiative in the development of elementary school teachers. They were a remarkable achievement, but they also had many inadequacies. The normal schools educated only a fraction of the needed teachers, and at a minimal level of training. They fostered the retention of only a small proportion of those teachers. There was constant and critical debate about the appropriate emphasis of normal school curriculum, whether it should be 'subject matter' or 'method.'[50] Eventually, though, the focus of teacher preparation shifted gradually away from 'subject of study' to child development.[51]

The pattern of normal school development from east to west also influenced the consistency of standards across the continent and enhanced the quality and control of teacher-training. Regardless of their apparent inadequacies, after 1860 normal schools were generally accepted as the proper institution for elementary teacher training. They were most notable for what they later became than for what they actually typified in the mid-nineteenth century. By the early 1900s, the need for elementary teachers reached critical levels as public schooling expanded. As increases in enrolment continued, some normal schools offered lengthier and more extensive programs of preparation. The normal schools adapted themselves to the changing economic and social conditions that expanded education, particularly in the United States, and through a natural evolutionary process of responding to increased complexity, they gradually became converted into teachers' colleges. [52]

After 1900: The British Columbia Scene

The first Normal School in British Columbia was established in Vancouver in 1901, followed by a second in Victoria in 1915. During the early years, the normal school training programs were very brief, though gradually the sessions were increased until four or five months became standard. In 1926 British Columbia instituted a course of one academic year (nine months). In 1930 the completion of Grade XII Junior Matriculation became prerequisite for entrance to the normal school.

Teacher education, typically described and practiced as teacher-training, was only marginally associated with the broader history of university education in earlier days. In British Columbia,the relationship was tenuous at best. Teacher training generally was not regarded as an activity of post-secondary education. In addition, a rivalry of long standing had existed between Victoria and Vancouver. Both communities were adamant that theirs was the more appropriate site for the province's university. The possibility that at some time there could be a plurality of universities in Canada's westernmost and only lately settled province was not considered seriously by any except perhaps a visionary or two. Teacher preparation simply was not an element of those early discussions about developing a provincial post-secondary education system.

The idea of a university for British Columbia had been proposed by John Jessop, then Superintendent of Education, as early as 1877. When that initiative did not come to fruition in timely fashion, Victoria and Vancouver High Schools embarked on alliances with McGill University of Montreal and began offering first-year university arts courses. In Victoria, the operation began in 1903. In 1906, an Act was passed incorporating the Royal Institution for the Advancement of Learning in British Columbia, which established the McGill University College of British Columbia at Vancouver and in the following year included Victoria College. By the time this institution was taken over by the newly founded University of British Columbia in 1915, students were being offered three years in Arts and Science and two years in Applied Science.[53]

The preparation of public school teachers was another matter and part of a separate discussion: "For quite thirty years after entering Confederation, British Columbia depended on securing teachers, trained or untrained, from some other part of Canada or from Great Britain."[54] In 1901, a Provincial Normal School for the training of elementary school teachers was established, but in Vancouver, not in Victoria. That circumstance would change, though, in just over a decade. On June 9, 1913, the Province formalized a contract with Luney Bros. Ltd., a Victoria contractor, for "the construction and completion of a new Normal School at corner of Lansdowne Road and Richmond Avenue, Victoria, BC"[55] The new school, which opened in 1915, was regarded by locals and by Department of Education proponents as a significant gain for the capital city. However, that same year, and in part as a result of the inter-city battle over the location of a university, Victoria College was closed by the government in favour of Vancouver's Point Grey site for the University of British Columbia. It was reopened in 1920-21 in Victoria's Craigdarroch Castle.

Victoria Provincial Normal School building prior to opening, with dirt road and no landscaping, 1914. Photo courtesy of UVic Archives, reference # 016.0601

For six years, Victoria Provincial Normal School was the only local opportunity for education beyond the public school system. Despite that, neither of the Province's normal schools was regarded as a post-secondary institution by other education authorities. That situation continued for many years. In a curiously self-deprecating 1939 report titled "The case for granting academic credit to teacher-training courses," Victoria Provincial Normal School acknowledged that:

> In the Normal School, as in the University Teacher-Training Course, some of the work cannot be regarded as of University calibre. A number of the courses given in Normal School do, however, parallel University courses, and are worthy of some undergraduate credit. The following are in this class, and are accepted by other universities for undergraduate credit: Educational Psychology, School Administration, Principles of Teaching, History of Education, Educational Measurement. Even though regarded very conservatively, the Normal School year might well be entitled to five units of undergraduate credit; that is, one-third of an academic year.[56]

The Senate of the University of British Columbia was not moved by this appeal, although it may have noted the Normal School's "First Year Arts requirement for admission to Normal School,"[57] Perhaps the onset of the Second World War delayed consideration of the Senate's reply, which appears only to have been received by the Normal School some six years later. S.J. Willis, Superintendent of Education, referred in a letter to H.O. English, Principal of the Victoria PNS, to:

> the statement sent to the University of British Columbia in 1939 asking for credit for some Normal School and Summer School courses. The request for credit was dealt with by the Senate in December, 1939 but was not approved.[58]

Recognition by the University may not have been the only barren front. There is no indication in the extensive early letterbooks of William Burns, principal of Vancouver Provincial Normal School, of any dialogue with his colleagues at the Victoria School. However, in several of his annual reports to the Superintendent of Education, Burns had requested that the government provide a permanent Vancouver Normal School building. He also argued for satisfactory facilities for a model school for the demonstration of teaching practice. Burns eventually secured both, but even then he may have been discomfited by the grand facilities and enviable conditions provided in 1915 for his school's Victoria counterpart. As Calam has pointed out, the government "had by 1915 completed in Victoria a superlative facility the size and sophistication of which, compared with its Vancouver counterpart, immediately attracted Burns' attention."[59] In his report of that year, Burns noted that:

> *The work of this session was particularly heavy, not only from the overcrowding of our classes on account of the large number in attendance, but also because all of these students were in the Preliminary Grade and entirely new to the work of teaching; hence much individual assistance had necessarily to be given to them. However, by the unwearying exertions of every member of the Faculty we were enabled to show good results at the end of the session.[60]*

The Vancouver School had enrolled 264 students that year, compared with an opening enrolment of 45 in Victoria. Burns did not want his Faculty's efforts to pass unrecognized, nor did he want the Superintendent to miss the fact that he perceived some gross inequities between the two schools. In his only apparent acknowledgment of the new institution's existence, Burns expressed his hope for what he perceived would be a more equitable situation:

> *We trust that the Department will be able to carry out some plans whereby the inequality of numbers in the two Provincial Normal Schools will be lessened. It is impossible for Normal School work to be satisfactorily done in a class of fifty when so much must necessarily depend on the observation of the teacher in charge, in regard to the ability, attitude to the work, and personality of the student.[61]*

From 'Beyond Hope' to Victoria

From the beginning, it was clear that the two normal schools would draw from different populations. The Vancouver School would enrol students from Vancouver and the surrounding area – the lower mainland and the Fraser Valley. Victoria Provincial Normal School, on the other hand, was to serve Victoria, Vancouver Island, and the interior of the province, a vast region loosely termed 'beyond Hope.' That descriptor has remained in popular use in a variety of contexts. It is perhaps an indicator of the rural/urban and Lower Mainland/Interior divide that persists in the province, created and abetted by the province's unique geography – a region marked in its southwest corner by the large, fertile Fraser River valley and adjacent areas.

A 1928 Department of Education dictum specified that "those attending the Victoria school come from Vancouver Island, the upper mainland (north of the 50th parallel), the coast islands, and the interior (east of Yale)."[62] The University of Victoria continues to be identified as the institution of choice for many students from rural British Columbia, though that image is changing rapidly with the proliferation of post-secondary institutions throughout the province, including the University of Northern British Columbia in Prince George.

Students from "the early days" were well aware of the population division on which enrolment in the two normal schools was based. Bill Cross (VPNS 1949-50) commented:

> Victoria [Normal School] was a little unique. Remember that its population was made up of people from Vancouver Island and, as they used to put it, those beyond Hope. So, they came from what were then quite rural areas, and they tended to go back to rural areas. But then, when they got here, they got captivated by the big city, too.[63]

John Robertson and Dorothy (Millner) Robertson, who later married, attended Victoria Provincial Normal School in 1945-46, the last year of the School's temporary World War Two home on the grounds of Christ Church Cathedral. Most of their compatriots were from the interior of the province. John observed that:

> Nearly everybody that was there was from Vancouver Island or the East and West Kootenays. They had to be, that was part of it . . . anywhere outside the Lower Mainland . . . Yes, a lot from Michel/ Natal. We had to get up and talk about our hometown. And I think there must have been about seven people from Michel/Natal . . . By the time they all spoke about Michel/Natal we knew where every outhouse was.[64]

Those rural origins were an important factor in shaping the many enduring friendships that developed during the Victoria Provincial Normal School's 40 years. The students attended for only a single nine-month period, but their bonds of friendship stretched for many years and over many miles.

The work that began in Vancouver in 1901 and in Victoria in 1915 continued until 1956, when the Province's two Normal Schools were closed in favour of university-based programs of teacher education. Both Schools were firmly established by the end of World War One, but they would soon be closely scrutinized and queried. From the end of the First World War years, these teacher-training institutions were the focus of increasing interest and challenge by a newly-at-peace populace and by a government intent on ensuring rigour and quality. In the mid-1920s, the province's public school system was placed under the microscope of a provincially appointed commission of inquiry – the Putman Weir Commission.

Notes to Chapter 2

[1] Seymour Sarason, Kenneth Davidson, and Burton Blatt, *The Preparation of Teachers: An Unstudied Problem in Education* (Cambridge, MA: Brookline, 1986), 19.
[2] Ibid., 18.
[3] David Munroe, "From Yesterday to Tomorrow," in *A Century of Teachers Education (1857-1957)* Harper, Charles (Montreal: McGill University Press, 1957) 79.
[4] Ibid., 78.
[5] Ibid., 225.
[6] Charles Harper, *A Century of Public Teacher Education.* (Westport, CT: Greenwood Press, 1939), 108.
[7] Ibid., 97-98.
[8] C.A. Richardson , Helene Brule and Harold E. Snyder., Ibid., 229.
[9] Charles Harper, ibid., 110.
[10] Charles Harper, ibid., 53.
[11] Charles Harper, ibid., 113-121.
[12] Thomas Flaherty & John J. Flaherty, *James Carter: Champion of the Normal School Movement.* (New York: Clearinghouse, 1974), 1-14.
[13] C.A. Richardson, Helene Brule and Harold E. Snyder., ibid., 227.
[14] Charles Harper, ibid., 20.
[15] E. Williams, *Horace Mann, Educational Statesman.* (New York: The MacMillan Company, 1937), 228.
[16] Robert Downs, *Horace Mann, Champion of Public Schools.* (New York: Twayne Publishers, Inc., 1974), 55.
[17] Charles Harper, ibid., 21.
[18] Ibid., 22.
[19] Jonathan Messerli, *Horace Mann: A Bibliography.* (New York: Alfred A. Knopf, 1972), 441.
[20] Ibid., 439 -440.
[21] Robert Downs, ibid., 39-40.
[22] Ibid., 45.
[23] Ibid., 50.
[24] Ibid., 50.
[25] E. Williams, ibid., 198.
[26] Robert Downs, ibid., 51.
[27] Ibid., 55.
[28] British Columbia, *B. C. Government News,* hereafter *BCGN,* (Victoria, May, 1956), 19.
[29] Burwash, Nathanael, *Edgerton Ryerson.* (Toronto: Morang & Co., 1910), 170.
[30] Harold Putman, *Edgerton Ryerson and Education in Upper Canada* (Toronto: William Briggs, 1912),232.
[31] Ibid., 232.
[32] Nathanael Burwash, ibid., 173.
[33] Ibid., 192.
[34] Harold Putman, ibid., 234.
[35] Paul Axelrod, "The Promise of Schooling: Education in Canada, 1800-1914." *Canadian Journal of Sociology* 24, 3, (1999): 428-431.
[36] David Munroe, ibid., 78.
[37] Nathanael Burwash, ibid., 174.
[38] Ibid., 174.
[39] Ibid., 193.

[40] Ibid., 174.
[41] Ibid., 193.
[42] Ibid., 10.
[43] Ibid., 13.
[44] Sir Eric James, Two Mottoes, in David Munroe, ibid., 25.
[45] Ibid., 80.
[46] McDonald, Neil and Alf Chaiton, *Edgerton Ryerson and His Times.* Toronto: (MacMillan, 1978), 113.
[47] Harper, Charles A., ibid., 95.
[48] Ibid., 96.
[49] Ibid., 107.
[50] Richardson, C.A. , Helene Brule and Harold E. Snyder., ibid., 230-231.
[51] J.H. Putman & G.M. Weir, *Survey of the School System,* (hereinafter Putman Weir), (Victoria, BC: Printer to the King's Most Excellent Majesty,1925), 196.
[52] Richardson, C.A. , Helene Brule and Harold E. Snyder., ibid., 232-33.
[53] *BCGN* 4:5, May 1956, 2.
[54] Putman Weir, 199.
[55] Contract document, British Columbia Archives (hereinafter BCA), GR0054, Box 36, File 517.
[56] _____. *The Case for Granting Academic Credit to Teacher-Training Courses.* Victoria, BC: University of Victoria Archives and Special Collections, RG No. 1980-056.
[57] Ibid.
[58] S.J. Willis, to H.O English , 9 November 1944. University of Victoria Archives and Special Collections, University of Victoria, Victoria BC, RG No. 1980-056.
[59] John Calam, Teaching the teachers: Establishment and early years of the B.C. Provincial Normal Schools, in Nancy Sheehan et al, eds. *Schools in the West: Essays in Canadian Educational History* (Calgary: Detselig, 1986), 78.
[60] *ARPS 1915*, 53.
[61] Ibid., 54.
[62] Department of Education, *Regulations and Courses of Study for Provincial Normal Schools 1928-9* (Victoria, Department of Education, 1928).
[63] Bill Cross 2002.
[64] John Robertson, interview with Vernon Storey 17 July 2002, interview 23m, transcript in interviewer's file.

LEARNING
TO TEACH

TEACHER PREPARATION
IN VICTORIA, BC
1903-1963

Chapter 3
A System Examined:
The Putman Weir Commission

In 1924, the Government of British Columbia commissioned J.H. Putman, Senior Inspector of Schools for Ottawa, and G.M. Weir, a professor of education at the University of British Columbia, to scrutinize British Columbia's public education system. The Commissioners' mandate was clear and sweeping. They were to undertake, on behalf of the Department of Education, "a comprehensive survey of the school system of the Province...to include a wide range of matters relating to the academic, professional, financial, and administrative aspects of the system."[1] The preface to the Commissioners' 1925 report hinted at what was to follow in its pages: "Our recommendations, if carried into effect, would result in a number of radical changes in the school system of British Columbia."[2] Putman and Weir commented further that "While we have seen much to admire in the school system of British Columbia, we have also seen some features which, in our opinion, deserve less favourable comment."[3] The stage was set for a review and report that almost certainly would be viewed by some as a sweeping indictment of the efforts of British Columbia's teachers and those responsible for their preparation.

A Measure of Public Education

The Putman Weir inquiry was intended by the British Columbia government to be a comprehensive task. The mandate of the Commission was specified in a set of 19 focus topics and questions to be researched, including three regarding the preparation of teachers:

14. How can a greater number of men be induced to enter and remain in the teaching profession?

15. How can a greater number of successful experienced teachers be induced to accept and retain positions in rural schools?

16. How can the normal schools be made more efficient?[4]

Putman and Weir's findings are reviewed later in this section. The Commissioners' report made it clear that the normal schools deserved a portion of "less favourable comment."[5] Although the focus of this discussion is primarily on developments in teacher preparation in Victoria, the 1925 report addressed the question of teacher training broadly in a document that recognized, assessed, and critiqued the operations of both the Vancouver and the Victoria Provincial Normal School.

The Putman-Weir report recognized some regional realities that would be noted again in other reports on education in British Columbia: "The diversity of educational problems demanding solution in British Columbia is intensified by the great disparity in the geographical, social, and economic elements characteristic of different areas of the Province."[6] Many of the Commissioners' comments related to the particularly rural character of much of British Columbia. Curiously, their remarks were sometimes quite inconsistent in regard to the balance of benefits and disadvantages relating to rurality.

The public education system in the province was still relatively young. It had been established in 1872 through legislation under which "the Superintendent, in practice, was the whole school system. He licensed teachers, appointed them, fixed their salaries, inspected them, authorized textbooks, fixed the course of study, and determined the holidays."[7] After 1872 there was a series of new and amended acts, the school system had developed and expanded, and British Columbia had become somewhat urbanized in a few areas, although it would remain largely a rural province for many years. In regard to governance, the Commissioners noted, "the school administration of British Columbia has developed in the direction of local control until its cities, district municipalities, and regularly organized rural sections have as

much voice in school affairs as the older provinces of Canada."[8]
They were not entirely sanguine about the growth of local control,
asserting that "if the children in remote districts of British
Columbia are enjoying average school advantages, they owe their
good fortune to a system of education, in some of its aspects,
highly centralized."[9] The Commissioners' comments on these
advantages, though, suggested that there was in fact a great deal
of disparity among various schools and districts. They observed:

> *buildings and environment of great variety and marked
> contrast . . . Some have ideal surroundings, but the buildings
> themselves are primitive and very small. Many are built of
> logs. Some are not larger than 15 by 18 feet with a ceiling just
> above your head . . . Some of these buildings are tidy and
> clean inside and some sadly in need of paint, whitewash, and
> soap.*[10]

Teachers of the day, some of whom we have quoted elsewhere
in this book, faced a great disparity of circumstances, recalling
them in conversations and writings as clear memories from a
distant yesterday. It was not at all clear from the Commission's
reported findings that these teachers enjoyed a broad base of
acknowledgement or support in their work. Throughout the
Putman Weir Report, the Commissioners' tone was caustic, though
ostensibly offset somewhat by positive comments that frequently
seemed patronizing or self-protective, such as their observation
that "the great body of public and professional opinion in British
Columbia is sound at the core. The great majority of teachers are
alive to their responsibilities and anxious to discharge their duties
with efficiency and zeal."[11]

The Commission, the Schools, and the Teachers

Commendations aside, the Commissioners were clear that they
had observed among British Columbia's body of teachers "too
numerous exceptions (probably found in any system), many of
whom seek justification for their professional indolence."[12] The
tone and substance of some of the Commissioners' observations
and recommendations regarding teachers and teacher education
might seem almost implausible to many of today's readers:

> · *There is an inherent conservatism in the minds of educators
> and schoolmen that shows itself in a reluctance to depart from*

cherished theories and practices in the educational field even when these have been scientifically disproved . . .

· Indeed, educational reform has often been pressed upon schoolmen through the protest of enlightened members of the laity whose viewpoints were less prejudiced than those of teachers had become through constant immersion in benumbing classroom practices . . .

· This state of intellectual torpor is markedly evident in certain sections and in many educational institutions of British Columbia and other provinces.[13]

In addition to the Commissioners' extension of their critique beyond the boundaries of the Province that had appointed them, neither British Columbia's educational administrators nor its teachers escaped their scrutiny:

· Like the poor (in thought), a certain class of pseudo-prophets, would-be sages, and dabblers in the field of educational theory we shall always have with us. Some of these will probably be officials who believe in creating as little disturbance as possible through administrative or academic reform. The official type of mind, with certain exceptions, is indeed likely to become as "rutty" and myopic in outlook as the hidebound formal disciplinarians. Only the persistent and enlightened pressure of public opinion can shame either class into forsaking false gods . . .

· Likewise there will always be a small number of teachers who resent being aroused out of their mental lassitude and self-complacency . . . the pious ejaculation of "being old-fashioned enough" is but a disguise to conceal ignorance and mental inertia under a veneer of assumed respectability.[14]

A reasonable reader might suspect that Putman and Weir believed British Columbia's system of teacher preparation to be marked by pervasive and systemic problems. The Commissioners concluded their section "Traditional Aims Manifest in the British Columbia School System" by noting in summary that:

The remedy for many of these conditions is discussed in the subsequent pages of this Report. By way of anticipation it might be added that a more adequate system of teacher-training, accompanied by a more comprehensive and thorough system of inspection and supervision, especially in the rural areas, would effect a distinct improvement.[15]

Throughout the report, the Commissioner's views on the state of teaching in the province's schools were expressed in quite a consistent manner, with seeming praise followed by sweeping generalizations. A section "Quality of Teaching in Assisted and Rural Schools" provides an example, beginning:

> *Much favourable comment might be made on the quality of the instruction observed in certain assisted and rural schools. Many teachers in these positions showed themselves alert, zealous in their work, studious, and anxious to profit from professional leadership.[16]*

That brief data-free note constituted the total of positive comment in this three-page section. The Commissioners then observed that despite "much favourable comment:"

> *A considerable proportion of the teachers visited, on the other hand, were remarkably deficient in both their academic and professional attainments. In the isolation of rural life they had apparently lost their studious habits and fallen into the rut of old-fogeyism, routine, and drudgery.[17]*

Throughout much of the Survey as it dealt with teachers, the writers adopted a perspective that at best might be termed 'damning with faint praise.' Their positive remarks often appear to have been inserted simply to deflect any assertion that they had been categorical in their statements, rather than to present a comprehensive and balanced picture of the public school system. As an example:

> *It is not the purpose of the Survey to imply that the teaching personnel of British Columbia contains a larger proportion of the latter type of teacher than is found in the other provinces. We have no reliable information on this point, and it may be that, from a comparative viewpoint, British Columbia is particularly favoured in the inspirational powers of its teaching force. It is the intention of the Survey, however, to point out defects, with a view to their betterment or elimination, rather than to praise the qualities of the many able teachers found in the schools of the Province.[18]*

The Report then noted, "The fussy, talkative teacher is too much in evidence in many schools."[19] It offered specific critical observations on teachers' tendencies to dominate classroom dialogue, and concluded the paragraph by asserting, "It is doubtful if a more successful method of stifling interest, blighting initiative, and discouraging real self-activity on the part of the pupils could have been devised by the schoolmen of the middle ages."[20] Despite that and similar observations, the Commissioners protested in summary that "our aim is to draw attention to the exceptional cases."[21]

The Commissioners were much concerned with the display of what they termed "formalism" and "discipline." In that era of an emerging emphasis on child study, they observed what they considered to be an over-emphasis on structure and rigidity, often evidenced by student posture, movement, and response patterns. Perhaps these teachers' classroom routines had been influenced by the physical training they had viewed at the Normal Schools, typically delivered by members of the military borrowed for the occasion. The Commissioners were sharply critical of classroom practice that often led to students assuming "a position of frozen rigidity or stilted immobility," suggesting that "such an attitude may become second nature to a Prussian bodyguard, but children should not be dehumanized to meet the requirements of a perverted notion of "discipline"."[22] The Survey recommended that:

Normal school instructors, inspectors, and supervisors should make a determined effort to eliminate or greatly reduce formal discipline in all its manifestations – as seen in the pupils' marching, posture, responses, and in the teachers' methods of instruction.[23]

The urban schools of the province did not escape the Commissioners' wrath. After descriptions of some unimpressive teaching, the Survey report suggested:

The only way that the public can eliminate these incompetents from the teaching profession is first to insist upon a high standard of normal school training, and second to insist upon adequate expert supervision of teachers-in-practice.[24]

Overall, the Commissioners were not impressed with circumstances in British Columbia's schools. In a summary comment, they singled out teachers for special attention, commenting particularly on three dimensions of their preparedness for the work: qualifications, professional development, and specialized training. Beyond castigating school people in regard to their pre-service preparation and continuing education, they doubted that these teachers had the capacity to improve, even with experience! Their final damnation carried no hint of faint praise:

Too many unmarried teachers; the immaturity of the teachers, especially in rural schools; lack of vision and professional pride; deficient academic and professional qualifications; unwillingness to take additional professional training beyond the legal minimum; lack of experience; inability adequately to profit from experience; tendency to change schools too frequently; lack of special preparation for teaching in ungraded schools; lack of sympathy with, and appreciation of, problems of rural life; dogmatism; lack of personality. The above list constitutes a strong indictment.[25]

Taken at face value, the Commissioners' overall findings regarding teacher preparation raised issues that had the potential to shake the province's system of teacher preparation to its roots. How would the two Normal Schools respond?

The Normal Schools in 1925

In 1920, British Columbia's Superintendent of Education had begun upgrading the teacher certification process, particularly the qualifications required of candidate teachers. The events marking that process were recorded in Putman and Weir's Survey, as was the Commissioners' tone and focus-setting observation that by the time of their 1924 review, the task of teacher preparation was "not yet complete . . . the normal schools are still in need of a thorough reorganization in aims, curriculum, and methods of instruction. Much has been done, but much remains to be done."[26]

Underlying many of the Commissioners' comments was a theme of concern for "mindlessness," which they saw as a widespread lack of grounding in either philosophy of education or then-current knowledge about child development and learning, which they referred to in the Survey as educational psychology. Associated with this was an over-emphasis on the learning by normal school students of "concrete definite methods," a theme that appeared to predominate and at least precede, if not replace, the study of educational psychology. This trend may have led to the Commissioners' detailed treatment and critique of the lecture method. In regard to the teaching of educational psychology, they suggested that "To attempt to teach psychology in this unpsychological manner is as futile as attempting to teach the use of educational tests and measurements by dictating the directions for the use of these instruments of diagnosis."[27]

Although they conceded the legitimate use of the lecture method, the Commissioners saw it as unreasonably predominant in the approach of many normal school instructors. By inference, they said, it would be reasonable to assume that neophyte teachers would carry this style into their own classrooms. In support of the Commissioners' efforts, it is helpful to note their call for a higher degree of reflectiveness and general thoughtfulness in the practiced craft of normal school teaching. They lent specificity to that call by recommending a more systematic and thorough use of available and current textbooks, an emphasis that had often given way to a stated concern for students' economic situations as a reason for not requiring textbook purchase.

The Commissioners concluded this section of their report with a set of 15 recommendations. While they did not end the section on the normal schools with a summary, an earlier summary comment offers insight into the fundamental view and attitude underlying their carefully qualified comments:

> *The above remarks may appear to constitute a sweeping indictment of the normal school faculties. We hasten to add, therefore, that it is not our intention to imply that all instructors in the two provincial training schools are slaves to the lecture method. Some of the lessons observed in these institutions impressed us as models of educational propriety; while others varied from very inferior to fair.[28]*

From a perspective of early 21st Century hindsight and distance, the Commissioners' disavowal of any intent to categorize the entire system of teacher preparation in British Columbia as falling far short of expectations lacks the convincing ring of truth. Time and the practice of later teachers and normal school instructors would be needed to indicate the extent to which the Putman Weir Commission had affected public education in British Columbia.

Recommended Action, Evidence of Response

Putman and Weir were sharply critical of practice in British Columbia's normal schools. The Commissioners expected to find creative laboratories for child study, institutions responsive to emerging trends in and knowledge about the educational development of children and the preparation of their teachers. Instead, they reported a scene they considered reminiscent of yesterday's practices, managed by officials from yesterday's scene. Putman and Weir asserted that:

> *Beginners ought to leave in possession of a philosophy of education as a guide to classroom practice. Instructors should deal with principles of educational psychology, not dictate notes on "tricks of the trade" . . . in sum, the ideal normal school had seven emphases: child study; ethics or social psychology; methods and curriculum; practice teaching; liberal education; social sensitivity; and physical health.*[29]

In the Commissioners' opinion, that was not yet the scene in British Columbia's normal schools. In fact, according to John Calam, the Schools did not measure up to Putman and Weir's conception of "an ideal normal school:"

> *Against this glittering image, B.C.'s normal schools paled by comparison. A few minimal reforms aside, said Putman and Weir, the normal schools' inexcusable aberration was their conception of teaching as a trade dependent on definite methods; thus definite instruction in these definite methods became their preoccupation. But, Putman and Weir contended, teaching wasn't a trade – it was a science. And since only this premise could justify any normal school's existence, British Columbia's normal schools should fall into line with it insofar as it affected their organization and administration, curriculum, ways of imparting knowledge, course duration and practice teaching.*[30]

Immediately, the question of response arises – how did the normal schools, and particularly the Victoria School, address the Commission's findings and recommendations? Beyond the careful analysis of Putman and Weir's work offered by Calam,[31] is there evidence of Normal School action in response? As I have noted, very little remains of the official record of the Victoria Provincial Normal School. However, for both schools, the Normal School

Principals' Annual Reports exist within the overall British
Columbia Annual Report on Public Schools. It seems reasonable to
expect that action taken on the basis of the Commission's analysis
would be documented in those reports. On the assumption that
any tangible response could be expected to occur within a
reasonable time period, I reviewed the Principals' Reports for the
period 1926 through 1930, the five years following the Putman
Weir Commission's investigation.

It seems reasonable to infer that the Commissioners'
recommendations would have intended to address the most
compelling areas of need. However, not all appeared to focus on
matters at the core of effective teacher training practice. For this
review, I examined three areas of recommendation that appeared
fundamental to the effective preparation of teachers: observation
and practica, faculty professional development, and curriculum.
Of these three areas, curriculum received the broadest emphasis.

Observation and practica

Debate around the appropriate mix of theory and practice has
raged throughout the history of teacher preparation. Overall, the
trend has been toward more extensive intern-style immersion in
the practicum experience. Despite the extension of the normal
school year from the very early days, though, Putman and Weir
were concerned that still not enough time was available either for
instruction or for observation and practice teaching. They
recommended that the normal school year be extended to 40
weeks.[32] Within that period, they proposed, there should be 50
hours each of observation and practice teaching. They listed seven
specific and essential requirements of the experience:

> That great emphasis should be placed on requiring a student-
> teacher to teach a class for a half-day or a full day; to plan
> and supervise seat-work; to teach a connected series of lessons
> in one subject; to use standardized tests in the "tool" subjects;
> to prepare maps, charts, sketches, and diagrams to illustrate
> lessons; to conduct organized games on the playground; to
> conduct a nature-study lesson out of doors; and to teach a
> series of lessons based on the "project" method.[33]

In this recommendation, the Commissioners provided a good
deal of specificity to support their assertion that teaching was

more than simply the delivery of lessons via the lecture method. The recommendation contained at least one sign of the impact of progressive education – encouragement for teachers to utilize the "project" method.

Faculty professional development

In a curiously modern manner, the Commissioners proposed that normal school faculty members, in the company of other supervisory personnel, should make frequent visits to a variety of elementary schools. Additionally, they suggested professional development visits to "training schools for teachers in other provinces or states."[34] In a clearly but not surprisingly patronizing manner, they suggested that some faculty school visits be "in company with inspectors or directors of education."[35]

Normal School curriculum

The Commissioners' recommendations regarding the curriculum of teacher training focused on textbooks and resources, emphasized specific subjects, and reiterated concern about the predominant use of the lecture method. In the first case, one might assume that the use of textbooks for courses was quite limited, since they proposed that "textbooks in each subject should be assigned."[36] In the second case, the Commissioners proposed a greater or revised curricular emphasis on educational psychology, educational foundations, and physical education. In the third case, the Commissioners captured their vigorous criticism of instructors' instructional style in their recommendation that "the present lecture method should be reduced to a minimum."[37]

One might expect that the Principals' Reports would address the Normal Schools' responses in these three areas. Since this research focused on the Victoria Provincial Normal School, my emphasis was on those reports. Shortly after the publication of the Putman Weir Report, Principal MacLaurin was absent for an extended period. His duties were assumed by Acting Principal Vernon Denton. Interestingly, virtually all comments that might be considered responses to the Commission's findings and recommendations were contained in Denton's 1926-27 report.

Vernon L. Denton, Acting Principal during Dr. MacLaurin's 1925-26 absence. Photo courtesy of UVic Archives, reference # 043.1105.

In today's context, one would expect that responses to a major public commission of inquiry would be detailed in the other major official record, the annual report of the system under scrutiny. In that regard, there is little to observe. The practice component did receive attention in the 1926-27 report:

It will be seen that there has been a marked broadening of the basis for practice-teaching. This has been brought about mainly through amendment to section 133 of the "Public Schools Act" and the lengthening of the Normal School term to the third week in June.

Each student received one week of observation and practice-teaching in our two-roomed Model School. This meant almost continual daily use of these rooms and threw a large share of the "breaking-in" process upon the shoulders of the principal, Miss Scanlan, and her assistant, Miss Barron. But the result, from the standpoint of the students-in-training, was most beneficial. The actual daily class-room procedure was seen and the students gained in poise, general class control, and in knowledge of sequence of lessons and of subject material.

Throughout the year, the number of hours of observation for each student has been materially increased; the number of lessons taught by each student have been more than doubled; the sequence of lessons has received careful attention; and the elements of control, of seat-work and its correction, the giving of tests, and the practical running of a school from day to day have been observed and tried out by each student-teacher. The practical side of the teacher-training course has thus been emphasized to a marked degree. Thee students have been given every opportunity to secure first-hand knowledge of teaching devices, the preparation and teaching of lessons, and the general running of a school from day to day.[38]

Only one other comment regarding the augmentation of observation and practice-teaching was entered in the record for the five-year period:

This continuous teaching and management has enabled the students-in-training more fully to appreciate the composite nature of the teacher's task and to apply their knowledge of educational principles to its best accomplishment.[39]

In regard to curriculum, one of the Commissioners' major Normal School emphases, the record is also sparse:

Mr. C.B. Wood took over the psychology, and by diligent application carried this difficult course through in a most satisfactory manner. In addition to this, Mr. Wood conducted a comprehensive course in mental measurements, objective testing, and achievement tests.[40]

In fact, the main reason for mentioning Mr. Wood's activities seemed to be as an indication of how Principal MacLaurin's duties were assumed during his illness. Mention of the physical education curriculum, though that was noted again in 1927, was similarly uninformative regarding Commission-inspired change, indicating simply that "The physical training was conducted by Sergeant-Major Bain and Sergeant-Major Frost. One hundred and fifty-nine students were awarded certificates in this course."[41]

There were no entries in the Victoria Provincial Normal School Principal's reports for the period 1926 to 1930 to indicate any other response to Putman and Weir's findings and recommendations. One can speculate regarding the reasons; perhaps extensive responses were recorded elsewhere, or perhaps the Principal's Report was not regarded as a valuable communication tool. One might also wonder whether the report actually resulted in any substantial action on the part of the Normal Schools. Be that as it may, these schools continued their predominant role in teacher training for another thirty years, shaping the classroom preparation and performance of thousands of British Columbia's elementary school teachers.

A Department of Education guide for Normal School organization, administration, and curriculum was issued in 1928.[42] It contained an extensive subject-by-subject list of reference books intended to support the teacher-training curriculum, which by this time consisted of 18 subjects, including some of the Commissioners' favourites: educational psychology, educational movements and sociology, nature study and agriculture, music and voice-training, and physical education.

Perhaps the principals were regarded primarily as managers of programs and curriculum prepared elsewhere rather than as curriculum leaders or designers. Certainly that would be consistent with many years of practice in regard to elementary and secondary school curriculum development in British Columbia.

The Normal Schools were islands of considerable consistency for many years. Undoubtedly they were seen by some as fortresses of overpowering rigidity. In terms of the history of Canada and British Columbia, they spanned a period that included two world wars, a major economic depression, and the social unrest and uncertainty surrounding each of these cataclysmic events. Whatever their strengths and weaknesses, and however lacking they appeared to be in the eyes of Putman and Weir and other critics, British Columbia's Normal Schools played a pivotal role in establishing, and in legitimizing as a vital social role, the teaching of British Columbia's children.

These first chapters have established an essential context for the more personalized text that marks the second part of the book. British Columbia's schools are human institutions, populated by real children and real teachers. There are many thousands of both, today and from years past, and no single book can be said to constitute "the record." I have become acquainted with just a few of the teacher-players in the drama. They have graciously agreed to share some of their memories with me and, in most cases, to share their stories and their identities with you, the readers of this book.

Notes to Chapter 3

[1] Putman Weir, 1.
[2] Ibid., v.
[3] Ibid., vi.
[4] Ibid., 2-3.
[5] Ibid., vi.
[6] Ibid., 14.
[7] Ibid., 16.
[8] Ibid., 18.
[9] Ibid., 19.
[10] Ibid., 20.
[11] Ibid., 43.
[12] Ibid.
[13] Ibid., 40.
[14] Ibid., 42-43.
[15] Ibid., 43.
[16] Ibid., 132.
[17] Ibid.
[18] Ibid.
[19] Ibid.
[20] Ibid.
[21] Ibid., 135.
[22] Ibid., 133.
[23] Ibid., 150.
[24] Ibid., 159.
[25] Ibid., 174.
[26] Ibid., 197.
[27] Ibid., 216.
[28] Ibid., 217.
[29] John Calam, 1986, 85.
[30] Ibid., 85-86.
[31] Ibid., 86-91.
[32] Putman Weir, 227.
[33] Ibid., 228.
[34] Ibid, 227.
[35] Ibid.
[36] Ibid., 228.
[37] Ibid., 229.
[38] *ARPS 1926*, 53.
[39] *ARPS 1927*, 52.
[40] *ARPS 1926*, 53
[41] Ibid.
[42] Department of Education, *Regulations and Courses of Study for Provincial Normal Schools 1928-9* (Victoria, Department of Education, 1928).

LEARNING
TO TEACH
TEACHER PREPARATION
IN VICTORIA, BC
1903-1963

Chapter 4
More Than a Building

The available official record of the Victoria Provincial Normal School is sparse. From the perspective of an archivist trying to assemble the elements of a history, it could almost be considered ephemeral. The files, copies of correspondence, and reports that one might expect to locate in regard to an important public institution with a 40-year history, are largely unavailable. Perhaps that is due to a disposal of records that might have occurred when the Victoria Provincial Normal School building was appropriated from 1942 to 1946 for use as a military hospital. On the other hand, perhaps the records disappeared when the Normal School was closed and its students became part of Victoria College in 1956. The latter seems more likely, since beyond a physical move, there had been no discontinuity in Normal School operations during World War Two. Perhaps the 1956 closure of the Normal School in favour of creating a college school of teacher education signified to someone with responsibility for an office move that an era ended could become an era forgotten.

Whatever the cause of the loss, an important sub-text of British Columbia's history is without much of the supporting data needed to construct a complete and credible record. Some items, primarily single letters, small collections of correspondence, and a few reports have survived, and the items entered in provincial government reports remain on the record. Among the items from officials who contributed to what now exists as a small collection in the University of Victoria Archives, only administrator Harry Gilliland's reports communicated any sense of historical development or even a partial record of events.

That shortage of material was not entirely problematic, though a greater repository of original documents would have been very helpful. The circumstance reminded me that often, the richness of our stories is found not so much in official lists and records as in the memories and memorabilia of those who were there. In the case of Victoria Provincial Normal School, the richness of the story was contributed by the student teachers who attended the Victoria PNS, a few of whom participated with me in this project. This chapter and the next three describe the School's operation and record some highlights of the memories recalled by those teachers, both while they were enrolled in their preparatory year and as they moved out into communities to practice their craft.

A Place to Learn

Except for a four-year period during the 1940s, the Victoria Provincial Normal School was housed in a dedicated building constructed by the Province in time to open for that purpose in 1915. In part, the building was constructed to ease problems of high enrolment in its Vancouver counterpart. Donald L. MacLaurin was appointed the first Principal. Earlier, in his annual report as Inspector of High Schools, MacLaurin had indicated his views of the important roles of both the public school and the teacher, a perspective that would enable him to communicate to Normal School students the vital nature of their preparation experience:

> The school is primarily for the pupil. The equipment, the organization, and the teaching are of vital importance. If lack of equipment, poor organization, or weak teaching is causing pupils to lose their time, it is too serious a matter to pass unheeded. The development of the youthful mind and character must brook no trifling. He who is unwilling to place the highest valuation on this work should leave untouched the office of trustee or teacher.[1]

MacLaurin was impressed by the Victoria Normal School's new home, noting in his report to Alexander Robinson, Superintendent of Education:

> Sir: I have the honour to submit this first report on the work of the Victoria Provincial Normal School.
>
> The school was opened to the students of the Province on

January 4th, 1915. The new and commodious building is located on a beautiful elevation in the north-east of the city, in a rapidly developing section. This site affords a panoramic view of the City of Victoria and the island-dotted Strait of Juan de Fuca that is of unsurpassed grandeur. The building contains, in addition to the usual offices and cloak-rooms, seven class-rooms for the Normal students, a library, reading-room, theatre lecture-room, chemical laboratory, physical laboratory, biological laboratory, art-room, sewing-room, cookery kitchen, household suite of rooms for the teaching of household science, manual-training room, forge-room, gymnasium, two recreation-rooms, two luncheon rooms, two shower-bath rooms (each provided with a plunge-bath), two classrooms for the Model School, and a large auditorium. The building is lighted with electricity, and has its own private gas plant for use in connection with the cookery kitchen and science laboratories. The interior finish of the building is of marked beauty. The auditorium is especially attractive. In all, this building bespeaks the forethought of the Department of Education and the importance attached to the work of education in the Province of British Columbia.

The session commenced with forty-five students in attendance. These were drawn from Victoria and vicinity, Kamloops, Vernon, Prince Rupert, Duncan, Chemainus, and Parksville. As the policy of simultaneously conducting Preliminary and Advanced Courses was adopted at the time of the opening of this school, these students were divided into two classes. Twenty-six took the Preliminary Course and nineteen the Advanced Course. Forty-one students completed the courses successfully . . .

To provide practical teaching for the students a two-division Model School has been located in the Normal School building. This is of especial value in that it affords to students an opportunity for observation and teaching in semi-graded classrooms. Here the students meet the actual conditions that will confront most of them when they first go out to take charge of rural schools...[2]

The principals of the Victoria Provincial Normal School were people of relatively long tenure in their work at the School. The first three served for 17, 12, and 10 years respectively. Although

Staff and first Victoria Provincial Normal School graduating class, May 1915   Photo courtesy of UVic Archives, reference # 006.0901. Photo by Savannah.

the fourth was principal for just the last two years of the School's history, he had previously served as the School's vice-principal for eight years. Harry Gilliland recounts the chronology that ended in 1956:

> The Provincial Normal School at Victoria opened its first session in January, 1915. There were eighteen students in the advanced course and twenty-six in the preliminary course. Its forty-second and final session was closed on June 15th, 1956.

> The first principal of the School was Donald L. MacLaurin, B.A., Ph.D., whose service continued from January 1st, 1915, for over seventeen years until October, 1932, when he was made Assistant Superintendent of Education for British Columbia. He was followed by Vernon L. Denton, B.A., D.C.L., whose term of office was from October, 1932, to May 24th, 1944. Harry O. English, B.A., B.S.A. was principal from September 1st, 1944, until August 4th, 1954. The writer was in charge from August 15th, 1954, until August 31st, 1956.

> The vice-principals of the School were: H.L. Campbell, B.A., M.Ed., L.L.D., September 1st, 1938, to August 31st, 1941 (made

Municipal Inspector of Schools for Victoria, now Deputy Minister and Superintendent of Education); H.O. English, B.A., B.S.A., December, 1941, to August 31ˢᵗ, 1944; Miss H.R. Anderson, M.A., Ph.D., September 1ˢᵗ, 1944, to July, 1946 (superannuated); H.C. Gilliland, M.A., September 1ˢᵗ, 1946, to August 14ᵗʰ, 1954.

The administration of the School continued in operation during the summer of 1956 to conclude its affairs...May this union be productive of great progress in teacher education. [3]

Victoria Provincial Normal School 1923.
Photo courtesy of UVic Archives, reference # 006.0608.

The history of the Victoria Provincial Normal School was marked for the most part by stability and, to the critic's eye, something of an aversion to change. It continued without a break in operation from its inception in 1915 to its absorption into Victoria College in 1956.

The School's first phase, under founding principal Donald MacLaurin, saw the establishment of a small school in a large building (much to the chagrin of the principal of the Vancouver Provincial Normal School), the coming and going of the First World War, a commission of inquiry into public education, and the first years of the Great Depression. The second phase, led by Vernon Denton, lasted through the remainder of the Depression and part of World War Two. During Denton's tenure, the building was seconded for use as a military hospital and the School moved to temporary quarters in Christ Church's Memorial Hall, where it remained until the end of the war. Principal Denton died of a heart attack during a Normal School year-end picnic in 1944. Harry English took over as the School's third principal in 1944, moved with the School back to its home in 1946, and remained in charge until 1954. On August 4th of that year, English too died suddenly, while defending his championship on the Uplands Golf Course. He had served much of his tenure as principal during the "shared years," the Normal School occupying one half of its building, Victoria College the other half. By the time Harry Gilliland became the fourth and final principal in 1954, it was clear that change was afoot. Just two years later, British Columbia's two normal schools would be closed in favour of a university-based approach to teacher preparation.

Early Years, War, and a Commission

Donald MacLaurin was born June 1, 1881 in Van Kleek Hill, Ontario. He gained his first degree, a B.A., from McMaster

University in 1904, the same year he was married to Nellie Evelyn Marchant. He taught mathematics in Victoria and moved quickly into school and school system administration, first at Victoria High School, subsequently as Inspector of Schools in the Kootenays in 1910, and Inspector of High Schools for the Department of Education in 1913. He began his 17-year tenure as founding Principal of Victoria Provincial Normal School in 1915.

Victoria Provincial Normal School building and students, 1955. Photo courtesy of UVic Archives, reference # 008.0619.

Donald MacLaurin was absent from his position as principal for an extended period beginning partway through the 1925-26 School year. Percy Wilkinson (VPNS 1926-27) was an early Normal School graduate, but because of MacLaurin's absence did not meet the Principal until some years later. Percy recalled:

> I had a very high respect for Mr. MacLaurin. He was a very fine man in all ways. He naturally was sensitive and concerned when the Putnam-Weir Report came out . . . He had been there, I think, 12 or 13 years, so . . . he took a busman's holiday, he went to the States where they had . . . new plans for education, the junior high school, intelligence tests, objective tests . . . And he went to England . . . France . . . Germany, and came back, having surveyed all the recent developments in education.[4]

The official record of the Principal's absence for the balance of the 1925-26 year observed that:

> Throughout the latter half of the school-year, staff and students alike regretted the enforced absence of Mr. MacLaurin. All were alike delighted that renewed health presaged his early return to his duties as head of the school.[5]

However, MacLaurin's return would not be as prompt as the Principal's Report had anticipated. In his report on the 1926-27 school year, Acting Principal J.W. Gibson noted: "Principal MacLaurin was unable to resume his duties at the beginning of the school year."[6] Although Gibson authored the Victoria School's annual report, it appears that by the time it appeared, MacLaurin had returned to full responsibilities. Gibson's final paragraphs allowed him an opportunity to record his "real pleasure to have had the opportunity once again of participating in the training of young men and women for the teaching profession."[7]

Donald L. MacLaurin, first Principal of Victoria Provincial Normal School, 1915 to 1932 Photo courtesy of UVic Archives, reference # 043.1113.

Anecho, the yearbook published while J.W. Gibson was Acting

Principal, was dedicated to him "in appreciation for what you, as principal, teacher and friend have done for us."[8]

Following his time as Acting Principal, J.W. Gibson was

appointed Inspector of Normal Schools, and in that capacity "had opportunity to observe the good features and also the shortcomings in the two Provincial institutions."[9] He is remembered for his efforts to develop the grounds of the Lansdowne campus through the grading and landscaping of

the grounds. Trees and flowering shrubs were planted in relation to the out-cropping of glaciated rocks . . . he hoped that every student would recall . . . the truly beautiful grounds with a sense of filial devotion. J.W. had found it a glaciated waste . . . He left it a park.[10]

John Wesley (J.W.) Gibson, Acting Principal of Victoria Provincial Normal School 1926-27, later Inspector of Normal Schools. Photo courtesy of Dr. W. Gibson

Following his return to duty, Donald MacLaurin continued as Principal of Victoria Provincial Normal School until 1932. In September of that year, he was appointed Assistant Superintendent of Education for British Columbia. His name has since been honoured on the campus of the University of Victoria, where the building that opened in 1967 to house the Faculty of Education bears his name.

Continuation and Displacement

Vernon Llewellyn Denton succeeded Donald MacLaurin as the second Principal of Victoria Provincial Normal School. After graduating from Acadia University in 1903, he attended the Normal School in Regina. He then taught in Saskatchewan and in Vancouver, B.C. where he became an Inspector of Schools before joining the instructional staff of the Victoria provincial Normal School and becoming its principal in 1932. Denton, an instructor of history and geography, is remembered in the province and elsewhere for his book, *The Far West Coast*, a record of the maritime exploration of the Pacific Coast, and for a geography text

Students gardening at Victoria Provincial Normal School, 1922.
Courtesy of UVic Archives, reference # 007.0001.

co-authored with Lord, *World Geography for Canadian Schools.*
Sadly, Denton died 'on duty' during a Victoria PNS student year-
end picnic at Willows Beach Park in May, 1944. Students of the
1943-44 class immediately established the Denton Memorial
Award, an annual presentation of a ring to the student showing
the best all-around qualities (teaching, academic, student affairs,
and athletics).

Vernon Denton left a lasting impression on Ken Bradley (VPNS
1926-27), a Normal School graduate who still recalled the
Principal's influence more than 75 years later:

> *A member of the faculty who made the most impression on me
> was Vernon L. Denton. And, his method of teaching social
> studies was absolutely tremendous. And in teaching it, I tried
> to follow his scheme of things. And, you know, the strange
> thing is, that I was criticized by one of the superintendents for
> doing that . . . making a topic so realistic that the impression
> lasted all your life . . . [Denton] was talking about rain clouds
> coming in off the Pacific hitting the mountains, and then
> raining, you see, when the moisture went up and condensed.
> And he acted it out, like a drunk man staggering towards the
> coast.*

> *Oh, yes, absolutely...this superintendent said to me, "You're
> just entertaining the class." He said, "The way to do Social
> Studies is to give them the textbook and a set of 20 questions,
> and they read the book and answer the questions." And I
> thought to myself . . . "How bloody dull."*

I went back to my way because I knew it was the right way. If I could interest them, it would last, and then they would want to read about the things. But how dull to have a textbook and a piece of paper and write things . . . [Denton wrote] a remarkable book on the early explorers of BC, the Spaniards and so on. And when I had used that in teaching, I tried to tell the class the way he told us. It was so dramatic. All these explorers, I know them as well as I know my own name.[11]

According to Joe Lott (VPNS 1941-42) and other students who remembered Denton, the Principal was a colourful character, a former sailor with an interesting talent:

You must have heard lots of stories about him. he was a pretty grizzly old devil. He would be teaching us something and he would go over to the side and throw up the window and spit out the window . . . he was just a real old style educator. I think he was raised in the Maritimes, I think he got his education there, not that that has anything to do with the window.[12]

Denton's aim, it seemed, was accurate. Beyond that, his humanity was an encouragement to some of his students:

Vernon L. Denton, Principal, 1932 to 1944
Photo courtesy of UVic Archives reference # 007.1102.
Ken McAllister photographer.

Dr. [sic] Denton . . . had been around enough to be quite a human, he was not the normal, sometimes intimidating, education professor . . . rumour had it that he sat by the window and spit out the window and referred to it as a "hole in one."[13]

Social events during the Normal School era were matters of protocol and decorum. Those in charge were interested both in a controlled atmosphere and in ensuring opportunities for all in their charge. Their ideas were not always well received by students. On one occasion Joe Lott's personal plans had been made, and he was not prepared to comply with expectations. Joe remembered:

I was called in . . . and told I was to take one of the Normal School girls or not attend the dance. Anyway, I went to see old V.L. Denton . . . apologetically, I said, "I've got this girlfriend, I've been going with her over a year," and I said, "I would like to take her to the dance, and I've been told I can't and have to take someone else." So, I said, "I'm not going to go to the dance if that's the situation." Anyway, gruff old V.L. got things straightened out and I took Rita [they subsequently married] to the dance.[14]

World War Two broke out during Vernon Denton's time as principal. Although Victoria was thousands of miles away from the action, both geographically and, for many, in conscious thought, things changed. Classes at the Normal School were predominantly female – Marjorie (Thatcher) King of the class of 1940-41 recalled that during the early war years:

Among the students there were only 10 or 12 boys, I think, in the class. There were about 90, and the rest of us were girls. War had broken out the September that we were in Senior Matric and a lot of the boys joined up that fall, right out of high school . . . And I expect that the reason for the small number of boys at the Normal School was that very factor.[15]

A minority male population characterized the Normal School throughout its existence, though it was even more evident during the War. As late as the Normal School's final year, Pat Floyd (VPNS 1955-56) recalled, "Our classes were divided, male and female, and the females outnumbered the males about three to one, if I remember."[16]

For some of the young men in the Normal School classes, going to war was not an option. Not all were pleased, though,

The male population of VPNS was very small after WWII began. Photo of boys class of 1940-41.   Photo courtesy of Marjorie King.

with what they saw as a limited perspective on the part of recruiters that resulted in their exclusion from military service:

> *A blind spot on the Armed services. I could have been a trainer of physical education, which I did in my high school teaching years, or I could have been involved in some aspect of transport. However, that was their rule, if you couldn't see down the sights of a rifle and hit a target, in those days, you were unfit . . . It was a blow to your masculine ego to be declared unfit for service, when you'd played sports and you know, as far as your physical body was concerned, you thought you were quite capable.[17]*

Though women had always been in the majority at VPNS, theirs was an uncertain role. Women were certainly valued as teachers, but the social norms of the day dictated that if they married, they would be required to leave teaching and occupy their place in the home. As is so often the case in human affairs, though, pragmatics would win over principle when a large proportion of the active male population was suddenly unavailable for classroom service:

> *Came the War, married women, anybody, could teach. They needed teachers, and that was when the matter changed. Married women were able to teach . . . I'm not sure when it*

VPNS faculty and staff, 1941-42. Front row: Muriel Pottinger (Secretary),
K.B. Woodward. Middle row: Percy Wickett, Isabel Bescoby, Barbara Hinton,
Marian James, Nita E. Murphy, Henrietta R. Anderson, Vernon L. Denton
(Principal). Back row: Sgt. Major Pocock, H.O English, John Gough. Photo
courtesy of UVic Archives reference # 004.0400. Ken McAllister photographer.

*happened. But [until then], it was a thing that women . . .
their place was in the home.[18]*

There was very little expressed disagreement that things were
meant to be the way they were up to that time, even though
certainly not all agreed. But patterns and regularities changed
drastically when the state of the world changed. For women such
as Norma (Matthews) Mickelson of the 1943-44 class, it was a
watershed period:

*Up to the time of the war, if you got married, you had to leave.
But, you see, when the World War came along, there were not
enough men around, so the war changed that whole issue, as
it changed so many other issues. I mean, women were not
going to put up with being told they couldn't be married and
teach after the war. So the war changed that, as well as a lot
of other things, as far as women were concerned – working,
being part of the working world, being able to do the job. But
up until that time, you didn't teach if you were married.[19]*

For Vernon Denton's about-to-be teachers, who by now were
ensconced in Memorial Hall, life was not really about war. World
events were far away. Though many had close connections to the

Anecho (VPNS Annual) staff outside Memorial Hall, 1944.
Front row: Mildred Young, Lois King, Michael Mikalishen. Back row: Wilfrid Johns, Norma
Matthews, Isabelle Godwin, Dr. Henrietta Anderson (Library Advisor), Patsy Galbraith,
Ursula Pottinger, Jean Bailey. Photo courtesy of UVic Archives, reference # 006.0001.

struggles through their families, life at school in Victoria during
those years seemed quite normal to Norma and her friends:

> We really didn't know what was going on over in Europe. We
> didn't have television, we had papers, and it was so far away.
> We were having a good time. We used to go out – invitations
> would come, and we would go out to Pat Bay, to the hangars,
> to the Navy place, and go to the dances. We were just having
> a good time . . . I was young, and life was good, I really knew
> that I was going to enjoy teaching. I did.[20]

Memorial Hall: "For the Duration and Six Months Thereafter"

In 1942, the Victoria Provincial Normal School's elegant
quarters were appropriated by the federal government for use as a
military hospital, to house members of the Armed Forces returning
from the field of battle for medical treatment and recuperation. A
move of unknown duration was necessitated, but limited quarters
were available in Victoria to house a multi-class program of this

size, and the Normal School's first interim location was less than suitable.

> *We were housed in the Sirocco Club and the offices were in the Memorial Hall, Christ Church Cathedral . . . in our later life, it became a popular nightspot in Victoria. I think we just used the big hall there, and there must have been a couple of smaller rooms that we used for other classes. I'm really fuzzy on just how we used the Sirocco Club. And I'm trying to remember when we went there. The Department of National Defence wanted a Veterans' Hospital and they took over the Lansdowne campus, and I think it was half way through the spring term that we just moved out and moved down there. It might have been at Christmas.[21]*

The move to humbler quarters was a sad reality of wartime life for Victoria Normal School staff and students. In her diary of that year, Lucille Hamilton noted that the students had "moved out of the Normal School today. Just another indication of wartime conditions – our lovely Alma Mater being torn apart. The staff feel quite badly...[students are] to be at the schools for 3 weeks then go to Shrine Cathedral."[22] Reflecting the mood of the times, she noted a few days later," Went up to Shrine Auditorium. Certainly is a comedown after the Normal School. No one minds of course."[23] Throughout, Lucille's diary recorded her thoughts regarding some of the World War II events that occurred in 1942 and the changed face of a once peaceful city now filled with uniforms and with a clear awareness that things were now different than they had been. Perhaps looking forward to her term-end return to Ta Ta Creek, Lucille commented "Golly it will be grand to be where I know people."[24] Two days later, she noted in her diary "Java is lost ... communication is cut ... My first day of practice teaching."[25]

In an effort to solve the problem of accommodating the Normal School, the Department of Education approached the Anglican Church with a view to securing larger quarters in Memorial Hall, an auditorium facility on the site of Victoria's Christ Church Cathedral. The Normal School's search for a longer-term temporary home that would accommodate its students and their programs, and the possible consequences of failure in this venture, were noted by the Executive Committee of the Synod:

> *The Department of Education had found it difficult to obtain a suitable building and had approached the Church-wardens of*

Christ Church Cathedral to obtain the use of a portion of Memorial Hall for which they would pay a suitable rent. It is very desirable that the Normal School should continue in Victoria and if a suitable place is not found to be available it would probably be transferred to Vancouver.[26]

That set of minutes also suggested that there may have been an internal communication problem between Bishop Sexton and the Christ Church Cathedral parish wardens. The Bishop stated "he was somewhat surprised that he had not been officially informed in regard to the arrangement being made with the Provincial Government."[27] Though Memorial Hall was located on the Christ Church Cathedral property, the owner, as for all Church property, was the Anglican Synod of the Diocese of British Columbia. The proposed arrangements had clearly violated Church protocol, and the matter was referred to the Synod's Finance Committee "for such action as it may think proper."[28] The Church Committee, though, had already agreed to lease the Memorial Hall space "for the duration and six months thereafter."[29] In the language of the day, "duration" was understood to mean "of World War II."

For several months, perhaps unknown to government and to Normal School officials, the lease arrangement was the subject of considerable internal Church correspondence and discomfort. Both the Synod and the Cathedral had legitimate interests. Each was concerned to guard the ownership of the Memorial Hall facility and to protect its tax-free status during the lease period. Both groups, though, seemed inclined to proceed with their patriotic duty. In a letter to the Synod's solicitors, Finance Committee Lay Secretary Fred Blankenbach described the arrangement as "a war effort by the Church."[30] Mutual interests were finally and formally recognized in a January 1943 internal Church document[31] that confirmed the August 1, 1942 lease agreement and acknowledged the Synod as owner of Memorial Hall. The facility was located on the grounds of Christ Church Cathedral, which occupied most of a city block in downtown Victoria. The Normal School occupied a portion of the facility as classroom, assembly, and office space until 1946, for a monthly lease fee of $250.00.

The students of the day recognized the needs and pressures of wartime. School life appeared to continue as in previous years, with little reference to the building that had been left behind for use as a military hospital. The Normal School was a unique social

Normal School students of 1945-46 and staff outside Memorial Hall Photo courtesy of UVic Archives, reference # 007.1707. Campbell Studio photographer.

microcosm, a stopping-place for students who enrolled en bloc, had no senior classmates, and except for the continuity offered by some instructors and administrators, had virtually no basis for developing an institutional history. Each new class of students arrived in September, most quite young and new to the area. They attended classes and observed in schools for eight months, then left both Normal School and city for their teaching careers. For fifty or more years in some cases, they gathered for class reunions to mark the passage of time and rekindle memories of that single year at the Victoria Provincial Normal School.

For the students enrolled during the Memorial Hall years, there were unique memories, most taken in stride by the students. John Robertson (VPNS 1945-46) recalled, "There was certainly no lunchroom. We used to eat in the boys' washroom, the men did, anyway. There was lots of room."[32]

In 1945-46, a marker for the end of the Second World War, there was a small ripple on the otherwise calm surface of the fall term. Several returning veterans arrived at Normal School a few weeks after the beginning of term. They were a group different in age and life experience from the Normal School's typical population. A student of that year recalled, "They were all wounded, they had all been wounded veterans... Some of them were limping a bit. Larry was on crutches for a while."[33] The returning veterans, also, faced a new and occasionally uncomfortable social scene. A more typical student recalled of his instructors and his fellow students, "I guess they had never been used to really having adults in Normal School – they were all like me, right out of high school."[34] Dorothy (Millner) Robertson

(VPNS 1945-46) noted that the new situation was perhaps somewhat more uncomfortable for some of the instructors: "It was just, they didn't really adapt to the fact that these men were veterans."[35]

This new population of savvy older students carried a different perspective on their new educational environment than did their younger colleagues, though they both recognized and appreciated the value of their opportunity to train as teachers:

I was four and a half years in the Air Force, and I found it almost a little kiddish, if I can say that. But, mind you, I wouldn't trade it for anything. It was wonderful. I don't think they treated me any different than the young kids. [36]

Some recalled their pre-war experience, the dreams and plans they had carried with them during the war years, and the reception they received from those who understood the maturing value of their recent experiences. Jim Whyte (VPNS 1945-46) remembered a strong bond with one of his instructors, a fellow former serviceman:

I had been to university before I went into the service, and I had always sort of looked forward to going into teaching. I always liked school, school was a wonderful place for me, and I loved it, and I did well, and I thought I would like to teach sometime . . . [We] were married during the war, in March, and I got out in August of '45, and I thought I would go to Normal School. And . . . I started Normal School the day after they sent us out on teacher practicum. I had never had any lessons or anything, just went out . . . I think it was a couple of weeks. I went to the Esquimalt school, Lampson Street. And Joe Hammett, one of the . . . instructors, had been in the RAF, and I had been in the RCAF, and he sort of took me under his wing. He liked me, we got along, and he told me, he said, "It's like bringing coals to Newcastle." That's what he said. "You shouldn't have to go for a practicum." I got along well . . . I didn't mix with many, we were expecting our first baby in December, my wife was still up in Nanaimo, and I didn't go to many of their dances or anything like that.[37]

The veterans enjoyed some modest benefits that helped to bridge their return to civilian life. In some instances, society formally recognized the value of their contributions:

Victoria Provincial Normal School Class "X" of 1945-46 in Memorial Hall gardens.
Photo courtesy of UVic Archives, reference # 016.0206. Campbell Studio photographer.

Now DVA, Department of Veterans' Affairs, had paid for me to go to Normal School. And then we got an allowance of about $90 a month, for my wife and I to live on. And as soon as we got through Normal School, it was cut off. And then I went on salary. The Greater Victoria Teachers' Association, they took up for the Veterans. And since I'd had four and a half years in the service, they took it up and said, you've got six years teaching now, or five years teaching now. So they gave credit. Some of the boys had to fight for it a little bit, but I didn't. I applied and I got it.[38]

For the regular Victoria Provincial Normal School students of 1945-46, this was simply their year to be trained as teachers. Though they differed from the students of prior years in terms of class composition, their aims were similar – to become teachers in the elementary schools of British Columbia. Their training facilities were modest, but the Normal School experience was to last for only a brief few months in this setting geographically close to, yet in other ways far away from, their nearest neighbours in education, the students of Victoria College.

From Cathedral to Campus

Harry Oswald English was vice-principal of the Victoria Provincial Normal School from 1941 to 1944. He was the School's principal for ten years, beginning in 1944 while it was housed in

Christ Church Cathedral's Memorial Hall. He was an athlete, a member of the University of Manitoba's Allan Cup winning men's hockey team during his university years. Following his tenure at the PNS, English served for ten years as a member of the University of British Columbia Senate, which recorded its sense of loss at his death on August 4, 1954. As had his predecessor, Vernon Denton, Harry English died suddenly of a heart attack while outdoors and engaged in recreational activity. The UBC Senate recorded its respect for the principal:

H. O. English, Principal, 1944 to 1954. Photo courtesy of UVic Archives, reference # 0603720212. Campbell Studio photographer.

Mr. English discovered and emphasized a man's good points. As Normal School Principal, he seemed to have a faith that each young person in his school could succeed; his convictions and personal influence were so strong that he, in turn, convinced prospective teachers of their innate powers, and encouraged them to tackle and to overcome their problems. The qualities most evident in his personality were those of modesty, faith, strength, determination, energy.[39]

This tribute from Harry English's fellow senators was consistent with observations made by some of his students, who remembered their principal's kindness and his concern and support for students. Bill Cross (VPNS 1949-50) recalled:

Oh, yes, he was . . . a most interesting fellow. He was really an educated farm boy, and he talked a great deal about farming as he taught his lessons. And indeed he took us to his garden to demonstrate gardening, in case you wanted to have a school garden.

The other interesting thing about Harry English – he would spot young men who came to Normal School who, in his view, weren't fitted out with enough clothing to go teaching. Because in those days, you wore a jacket and tie. And he maintained from his friends and others a huge wardrobe at his home. And he'd take you home, give you a sports jacket, or a suit, shirt, tie, the whole bit, so that when you went into your practicum you looked professional.[40]

Boys' Basketball team with coaches, 1949-50. Front row: W. Bowater, D. Henderson, W. O'Brien, P. Salva, D. Stainton, P. Pezel, G. Munro. Back row: Bill Cross (Manager), R. Kirby, K. Wright, R. Wayling, E. Oakley (Captain), Mr. Farquhar   Photo courtesy of UVic Archives, reference # 006.0306. Bill Halkett photographer.

English's kindness was not always the result of careful pre-planning. He was sensitive to other critical needs of some of his students, including Anne (Daser) Walters (VPNS 1951-52), who on her arrival from a tiny rural community unfortunately selected a boarding place that very quickly turned out to be highly unacceptable. Harry English heard of her plight and recognized how much she needed support, encouragement, and practical help:

> *Oh, Mr. English, who was the principal of the school, was a wonderful man. When I did this abrupt switch of boarding places, he called me in the next morning, and talked this over with me. The unhappy landlady had already called him to complain of my abrupt departure, leaving her without a babysitter. [Mr. English] told me how to get a student bursary loan, and not to worry. And he was encouraging me, "Look at your marks that you got in high school, you're going to do fine." He was a great person.[41]*

Often during the interviews, former students would recall their own personal encounters, not only with Harry English, but also with other professors. In a conversation regarding another of the administrators, John Jackson (VPNS 1943-44) went on to speak of English:

Dr. [sic] English . . . he would bring in a stack of books and say, So and so says such, so and so says such. I said to somebody going up the stairs that I found this very frustrating, and Dr. English [sic] was behind me, and he says, "Can I see you in my office later? . . . I felt the same way in school." I went to his office, we had a very pleasant talk . . . and he says, "I was frustrated with education and what was going on, too," he says. We were good friends . . . more than just teacher-student.[42]

John was not the only interviewee to bestow a doctorate on one of the Normal School faculty members. In some cases perhaps they confused Harry English with Dr. J.F.K. English, another British Columbia educator. In other instances, such as the references of some to Vernon Denton, they may simply have been offering professorial respect of a sort that was not universally offered by her colleagues to, for example, Dr. Henrietta Anderson.

Myths and legends abound in the annals of organizational history. Many cannot be substantiated, but some have a plausible

Dr. Henrietta Anderson Vice Principal of VPNS 1944-46   Photo courtesy of Mary Harker.

ring when considered alongside other evidence. Dr. Henrietta Anderson, vice-principal of VPNS for the first three years of Harry English's tenure, was the subject of one of those probabilities. In casual conversation, an interviewee who attended Normal School in the mid-1940s mentioned Dr. Anderson's comment to him that early in her tenure as an instructor at the Victoria Provincial Normal School, an administrator of the day had suggested that "Probably a little lady like you would not want to be called Doctor." According to the informant, Dr. Anderson had indicated quite clearly that "Doctor" was precisely the correct salutation!

On the face of it, that is simply an interesting and perhaps unverifiable anecdote. However, its credibility is enhanced in Harry Gilliland's own file record of the VPNS principals and vice-principals. There, the relevant entry is clearly titled "Miss Henrietta R. Anderson,"[43] even though further down that page her three degrees are listed, including her Ph.D. (1931) from the University of Washington. In fact, even in his "Brief history of the Victoria Normal School,"[44] Gilliland persisted in his decision not to speak of "Dr. Anderson." Despite his own listing of this woman's earned Ph.D. among her qualifications, he identified her in the official record simply as "Miss." Elsewhere in the report, though, he acknowledged the Deputy Minister of Education's honorary doctorate by referring to him as "Dr. H.L. Campbell." Historically, Gilliland's mention of Donald MacLaurin's doctorate in the record of MacLaurin's tenure as first principal of Victoria Provincial Normal School was also inaccurate. MacLaurin received his doctoral degree in 1934, two years after leaving the School.[45]

Former students' memories in regard to Dr. Anderson were remarkably clear. Without exception, they both knew and referred to her academic qualification. Joe Lott remembered a lively personality and an effective teacher:

And then we had Dr. Henrietta Anderson, who I am sure you've heard about. She was a real character, but a heck of a good teacher. She was really an inspiration.[46]

Marjorie (Thatcher) King (VPNS 1940-41) was particularly clear about the formalities of address in the 1940s, especially in regard to those in positions of authority or seniority:

We all liked her, as far as I know, but nobody ever thought of calling her anything but [Dr. Anderson]. You know, in those days, we called everybody Mr. or Mrs. or Doctor . . . like Dr. [sic] Denton, we called him Doctor, and there was Mr. English and Mr. Gough, and Mr. Wickett.[47]

In several cases, the mention of an instructor's name triggered an interviewee's memory of an experience involving that person. Often the memory focused either on a particular quality of the instructor or on a once-embarrassing moment to remember. For Norma (Matthews) Mickelson on one occasion, it was the latter:

I was at North Ward, my first practicum. My first supervisor was Dr. Henrietta Anderson, and I can remember, I was

*supposed to be teaching a Science lesson. I will never forget it
. . . it was a methodology course, it was how to teach things.
And I was going to have the kids plant peas. We were going to
plant peas, and they were going to watch these peas, and
water them.*

*Well...the class was at one level, and then there was a slight
rise to where the teacher stood - it was kind of like one step up
. . . And I was up on that little platform there, and
Dr. Anderson walked into the room, and I was so nervous, my
hands relaxed, and my bottle of peas fell on the floor and went
in a hundred different directions! Every kid in the room leapt
up out of his or her seat to pick up those peas. I will never
forget that experience![48]*

Dr. Anderson was a member of the instructional staff at
Victoria Provincial Normal School from 1934 until her retirement
in 1946. Among the six administrators appointed to lead the
School between 1915 and 1956, she was the only woman. She
was also the only VPNS administrator to hold a doctoral degree
during her tenure at the School.

Henrietta Anderson was born in Aberdeen, Scotland in 1885.
Dr. Mary Harker, recently retired from her work as an instructor at
the University of Victoria, Faculty of Education, recalls warm
memories of this family friend of her parents' generation,
capturing conversations she remembered:

*Her father was the principal of Aberdeen University, and from
the moment she had any consciousness she realized she
wanted to be a teacher, was driven to teach, wanted to teach
badly. And when she was a young person, she was the most
lackadaisical student you could ever imagine, she said. She
was bored out of her wits, she couldn't care less. She loved to
read, she was a voracious reader, and knew and quoted easily
and often from anything from Chaucer to T. S. Eliot. She was
amazing.*

*She often told this story; they had to write some kind of
matriculation exam in order to get into the Teachers' College . .
. she was living in typical adolescent [dreamland], not caring
a hoot about her studies and reading happily away. And her
father said to her, "You're never going to get to be a teacher,
you haven't got the marks," and it never occurred to her that*

*there was any question. And she said, "What do you mean?'
And he said, "You're not going to pass . . ."*

*And so then she started . . . she used to go to sleep every
second night, and she'd boil tea on this heater in her room, to
keep herself awake. And she often talked about that, and she
recapitulated all these subjects that she had to know, and . . .
didn't even care about . . . to become a teacher. And she
worked and worked and worked at her math, which was her
failing. . .and did well enough and went into Teachers' College,
and became a teacher . . . And then her first assignment was in
the east end of London, which I think she found very hard, but
very, very interesting.[49]*

Mary Harker remembers Henrietta Anderson as "animated and
lively. She was really a wonderful person to have around. And she
was always the life of any conversation that went on in our
house." She was not one to dwell on her own adversities, which
included stepping off a steamer in Halifax in 1912 to discover that
her life's plans had fallen through, leaving her abandoned and
having to make her own way in a new country. Undeterred, she
continued on as a single woman in a man's world to make
contributions that might been impossible for her had she been
married. She became a school administrator in the Vancouver area,
serving as the first woman principal of South Vancouver
Elementary School and subsequently as principal at Lonsdale and
at Queen Mary. She received her B.A. degree at Queens in 1925,
the Master of Arts in 1929, and the Ph. D. in 1931, the latter two
from the University of Washington. In 1934, she joined the faculty
of Victoria Provincial Normal School as assistant professor
Dr. Henrietta Anderson. From 1944 to 1946, during the Normal
School's period at Memorial Hall, she served as vice-principal
under Harry English. On her retirement, she was succeeded in her
position by Harry Gilliland. In 1954, Gilliland became principal for
the final two years of the School's operation.

Henrietta Anderson was a driving force in her community,
collector of an impressive array of "firsts:" the first teacher to
become President of the British Columbia Parent-Teacher
Federation; first winner, in 1932, of the Fergusson Memorial Award
for her outstanding contribution to the field of teaching; and
founder of Victoria's Silver Threads Society. She was an advocate
for improved teaching conditions for British Columbia's rural

schools, which faced perennial and systemic problems of high turnover, low salaries, poor equipment, and isolation. In 1949, retired and working with others, she revived the local Music Festival.

Henrietta Anderson raised an early voice on behalf of trades education for high school students, noting, "A university education is not in itself a passport to success or happiness...We must inculcate the ideal that all labour done well is dignified."[50] In a perceptive comment on social reality, she regretted,"It is a sad commentary on our system that the quickest way for pupils to get good trades training is to get sent to one of our correctional institutions."[51]

Where school sports were concerned, she was an advocate of broad participation, once observing: "There have been times when as principal I would have liked to dump the whole lot of silverware into the inlet."[52] An enthusiastic participant herself in all of life, she urged other women toward action: "If we are seeking equality, we must produce equality. Let us stand by each other and be all

Girls' Basketball team, 1945-46. Members: Frankie Boyes, Sheila Stuart, Connie McMechan, Margaret Morrow, Dorothy Millner (Robertson), Dorothy Villers, Rachel Woodward, Betsy Cook, Jean Bale, Lorraine Dwyer, Rozella Poulin, Miss Perry (Staff Advisor)   Photo courtesy of UVic Archives, reference # 006.0414.

for women and for all women."[53] Perhaps her commitment to service was captured best in her remarkably John Kennedy-like observation a few months before the start of the Second World War:

> I don't see any hope for a great Canada until we see more and more of our young people imbued with the ideal that they have a contribution to make to our country.[54]

Perhaps Henrietta Anderson carried that hope with her as she retired from Victoria Provincial Normal School in 1946. She continued her active and contributing life in Victoria until shortly before her death in 1968 at the age of 83.

Days of Discontent, Decade of Coexistence

Victoria College continued to be housed through the War years in Craigdarroch Castle, a facility that had been useful since 1921 but that was rapidly becoming too small. With the 1946 infusion of returning military personnel, the College's student population now numbered about 600. War's end and the looming repatriation of the Victoria Provincial Normal School building from its hospital status, coupled with the space requirements of the College, led to proposals to reconfigure or reassign the Normal School building's use. In the spring of 1946, Harry English, the Normal School Principal, expressed his concerns in a letter to Superintendent of Education Col. F. T. Fairey. Referring to a recent meeting with Col. Fairey and College president Dr. Ewing, English stated:

> When we explored the possibility of housing both the Normal School and Victoria College in the Normal School building, I came to the conclusion that nothing remotely resembling a teacher-training programme could be provided under the conditions that would prevail if we crowded both institutions into that building.[55]

English, in phrasing that may have foreshadowed the tenuous relationship between College and Normal School, and in fact between himself and Ewing, that would characterize the next decade, expressed his views forcefully:

> Perhaps I did not make my position clear on the question of my "willingness to cooperate"...I wish to make a brief statement regarding my attitude toward this whole problem.

*In the first place, I am a civil servant and as such believe that
it is my duty to place the welfare of the Department and the
rulings of the Department ahead of my personal desires. When
I can no longer subscribe to this stand, I have only one
alternative, namely, resignation.*

*As regards co-operation with Dr. Ewing [Victoria College
principal] under the circumstances which he outlined – that is
a different matter.[56]*

The letter from English to Fairey offered a further clue to the
Normal School Principal's angst, a disagreement that may have
had its roots in a long-standing difference of views regarding the
academic status of teacher-training programs. He pointed out to
the Superintendent of Education that:

*During our conference, Dr. Ewing insisted that if the Normal
School and Victoria College were merged in the Normal School
building, the Normal School would have to become a branch
of the College. Under those circumstances he assured me that
he would recommend to his Council that I be given the status
of an Associate Professor, but he could not be certain that the
Council would approve his recommendation, because I do not
hold a degree in Education.*

*It was interesting, to say the least, to learn that members of
the Faculty of the Normal School, all of whom are civil
servants, would be dependent for their status upon the
recommendations of an employee of Victoria School Board.
Under these circumstances, I do not think that I should be
expected to pledge a willingness to co-operate with the
representative of Victoria College, until the relationship of the
two institutions has been clarified.[57]*

The Superintendent's reply is not extant, but English's letter
was perhaps an early indication of the tenuous relationship that
prevailed between the two institutions until the 1956 closure of
the Province's normal schools.

For a period in 1946 just before a Solomon-like government
decision regarding use of the Normal School building, the matter
of classroom accommodation for the students from Victoria PNS
and Victoria College was the subject of open and vigorous dispute.
Victoria College had grown rapidly, swelled to a great extent,
albeit temporarily, by the end of World War Two and the return of
military personnel to civilian life.

As part of his 1946-47 welcome to Victoria College students, their Principal Dr. J.M. Ewing apologized in an address that clearly alluded to the College's recent efforts to secure space in the Normal School building:

> *I am ashamed to bring you into buildings so unsuitable for your reception . . . buildings whose accommodation is makeshift and wholly inadequate . . . No individual can be blamed for the situation in which we find ourselves, least of all the administration of the college.*
>
> *I must in all honesty and justice tell you that the administration has been encouraged to cherish hopes that have proved delusive, and has been prevented by these reasonable hopes from making preparations that should have been made six months ago. As matters stand, and dreadfully handicapped as we are, we are nevertheless straining every nerve to make the work of the college possible.*
>
> *The higher education of some 600 people, among whom are 250 returned men and women who have earned the gratitude of their countrymen, is to us a task of superlative importance. With your co-operation and forbearance, we shall carry it out despite all obstacles . . . It may comfort you to hear, though it will be cold comfort enough, that the faculty is suffering with you. Staff offices will be crowded beyond the limits of endurance, and the work of personal consultation, so vital to staff and students alike, will be carried on only under the greatest difficulties . . . Let us be courageous, hard-working and reasonably patient; let us pull together with all our might, and there is no doubt of our eventual success.[58]*

Background discussions had undoubtedly been taking place, as evidenced both by the English-Fairey exchange and by the College Principal's comments. Those discussions were referred to in a prepared statement from the Greater Victoria School Board noting that:

> *The present existing conditions at Victoria College have been known to the Greater Victoria School Board for some considerable time. Action, however, was taken by the board as far back as July, 1945, when the Victoria Chamber of Commerce, in consultation with the board, presented to the provincial government a brief suggesting that an exchange of*

*buildings as between the Victoria College and the Normal
School be effected. In May of this year, the deputy minister
was contacted by the board again with a view to effecting the
exchange, and the board was advised that the matter was
receiving the close attention of the minister. Dr. Ewing had
kept up continual contact with the board and was assured
that the board was doing everything it possibly could to direct
the minister's attention to what would become a serious
condition upon the reopening of the college . . . With reference
to the offer of the government to make available some
accommodation at the Normal School for part of the college
student body, the faculty spent a whole evening trying to work
out a time-table, but the principal had to finally report to the
board that the scheme was impracticable . . . The two
buildings are over two miles apart, transportation between the
two would have to be arranged and in addition it should be
borne in mind that there are not science laboratory facilities in
either building, so that the High School labs would have to
continue in use and the staff would be faced with the
impossible situation of trying to carry on in three separate
buildings at widely scattered points.*[59]

The Victoria Fire Chief now stepped into the fray, demanding
that several hundred students be moved from Craigdarroch Castle.
The City Health Department ruled that the Castle had insufficient
sanitary facilities. A newspaper article referred to the clash of
expectations in an article headed "Fire would cost 50 lives:"

*Victoria College students, including 250 men who had fought
for their country in the war, felt very badly when the school
term opened to find they had to return to the old Craigdarroch
building. They had been given to understand that they would
have the Normal School, capable of handling 800 students.
Normal School, however, was handed back to 125 students.*[60]

Banners from a College student march captured the flavour of
the debate: "Into the College of death filed the 600," "Never has
so little been denied so many by so few," "The Normal or
nothing," and "The government says nothing is too good for the
Veterans. Gentlemen, they mean it, we've got nothing." For the
College students, the solution was simple and at hand, just
"asking the government to have the College and Normal School
exchange buildings."[61] Principal Ewing was clear about the

College's ability to respond promptly to an affirmative decision by the provincial government, observing that "If we are given new quarters today, we can move over the long weekend and be prepared to start classes there by Tuesday."[62] Clearly, outside intervention was needed – it came in mid-October:

The entire student body, staff, and equipment of Victoria College will be moved from the Craigdarroch building to the Provincial Normal School building on Richmond Avenue, it was announced today by Premier John Hart. The Premier said alterations in the Normal School building, necessary for housing the college, will start immediately and will be completed in from three weeks to one month. The Victoria College will share the Normal School building with the Normal School's student teachers. The former Dunsmuir Castle, home of Victoria College for several years, will be abandoned by the college.[63]

The Victoria Provincial Normal School building was opened in 1915 as a dedicated facility for the preparation of teachers. Yet it would now accommodate a second tenant with a much larger population than that of the Normal School – Victoria College. From the fall of 1946, the two institutions shared what is now known as the Young Building of Camosun College's Lansdowne Campus. Despite the Department's decision being contrary to his preference, Harry English remained Principal of Victoria PNS until 1954, the year of his death. The Normal School-College relationship remained one of joint occupancy until 1956, when both Normal Schools were closed. Throughout, the two institutions operated under separate administrations, avoiding the need to determine either a structural relationship between the institutions or an academic rank for Principal English.

Signs of the building's wartime use remained when students returned in 1946: swinging doors, operating room lights, and in particular, a characteristic odour. Frank Gower (VPNS 1946-47) recalled the legacy of the Victoria Military Hospital:

It had been used as a military hospital, and it smelled like it . . . There was quite a cleanup necessary to try to get rid of the odor. The soup was made in what had been the operating room . . . it took a while for the odour to go away . . . it was not quite pleasant.[64]

The grand building that had been designed and built as an educational institution carried for years the marks of its temporary wartime status as a place of treatment and recovery for military personnel. Bill Cross (VPNS 1949-50) attended Normal School four years after the end of the war. He remembered an institutional scene:

In the Science lab, in particular, it still looked like you were in a hospital laboratory. And in the Art room the walls were still tiled and it was like having an art room in a biffy. And it had been the operating theatre. But it had lots of good light, and the fellow who taught us Art, Wilf Johns, just loved it in there.[65]

The two groups of students occupied different ends of the building, College in the west end and Normal School in the east end. The two cultures, also, were markedly different – prospective teachers present for a short program of pre-service preparation and College students bound either for university or for careers in a wide variety of fields:

The College students were only there for two years, the Normal School students were only there for one year, so they never really had any feel for that kind of thing at all. The Normal School students who were just there for one year, and mainly from out of town, didn't care, didn't know, didn't realize that the College had marched out there, in whatever year they marched on the place, and taken over, demanded some space.[66]

The separation persisted throughout the entire time of joint occupation, a subtle but systemic underlying separation not just between two ends of a building, but between two quite different cultures. In the eastern half resided a group of Normal School students uncertain of but in most cases relatively unconcerned about their status as post-secondary students. To the west was a group of College students undoubtedly aware that they were affiliated with but not really part of the University of British Columbia. The rivalry extended in some cases to tensions between College and Normal school faculty. Perceived differences regarding the relative academic respectability of Normal School and College referred not only to the two student bodies, but also in some cases to faculty members. Pat Floyd (VPNS 1955-56) captured the essence of the divide between the student groups:

We were at one end of the building and they were at the other end of the building...We were in the east, yes, and there was no or very little social communication arranged between the two groups. On a personal level, of course, it existed. In my case, because I graduated from Esquimalt High School, many of my former high school mates were in the College. And that was true of all of us in the Victoria area. It was also true of what we called the "beyond Hope" contingent, the people from the Interior who came down either to the Normal School or Victoria College – Normal School because they all came here, they couldn't go to Vancouver Normal School. But there was the odd person from the Interior attending the College as well, and so there would be a connection there, on a personal level. And there was some dating back and forth, inevitable that that would occur. But there's nothing that I can recall that was structured, in any way that would bring the two groups together... Two separate institutions, definitely, at that time.[67]

Dorothy (Millner) Robertson recalled some interpersonal tensions between the two groups of students and faculty, noting that "Looking down one's nose at Normal School, that was very evident,"[68] and that "There were some distinct animosities between personalities in the College and from the old Normal School group.[69] Bill Cross (VPNS 1949-50) offered a specific example:

And one of the people who carried on that animosity later on (because many of us went to Normal School and then completed our degrees through Summer Session) was one of the history professors, who definitely made it known that if he had teachers in the class, he felt that they weren't real students. And, I mean, he was nasty about it, and so nasty that, when I had to take a History course from him, along with three others, we walked out. And we went to the principal and explained to him that we couldn't stay in that kind of an atmosphere where he had already assumed we were stupid.[70]

Time has the capacity to fade memory. It can also mask a revisionist approach to presenting the historical record. The Victoria Provincial Normal School had opened and moved into its dedicated facility in 1915. That year, as noted above, a Victoria-Vancouver dispute over the best location for a British Columbia university came to a head with the provincial government's decision to locate the province's degree-granting institution at Point Grey in Vancouver. Victoria College was closed as a result, and for the next six years it did not exist. The Victoria Provincial Normal School was the sole and continuous occupant of its own building from 1915 until 1942, when that facility was seconded for use as a military hospital.

Only in 1946 did the Normal School and Victoria College begin to share the now reclaimed building. However, the reality of the building's history and its original status apparently was either overlooked or ignored by the 1985 narrator of a Camosun College videotape, who stated incorrectly that in 1946 "the building was returned to its original function as a college, this time for 600 students. The Normal School shared the facility with Victoria College."[71] In another synopsis of the history of Victoria College, the record is more accurate:

In 1946 the College moved from Craigdarroch to the Lansdowne campus of the Victoria Normal School. The Normal School, itself an institution with a long and honourable history, joined Victoria College in 1956 as its Faculty of Education.[72]

VPNS faculty and staff, 1953-54. Front: G.D. Tuckey, D.M. Daniels, R.M. Baker (Christie), W.A. Copeland, M.A. Hoey. Back row: H.C. Gilliland, F.H. Johnson, H.O. English, G.A. Brand, D.B. Gaddes, W.A. Johns. Photo courtesy of UVic Archives, reference # 006.1402.

Upon Henrietta Anderson's retirement, Henry ("Harry") Gilliland became the vice-principal of VPNS. He remained in that position until Harry English's death in 1954, after which he was appointed Principal. Like Harry English, Harry Gilliland was born on a prairie farm. English was born in Manitoba; Gilliland was a Saskatchewan product. He moved to Victoria as a child, and completed high school there. He was himself a graduate of the Victoria Provincial Normal School. He continued on for further education at the University of British Columbia, receiving a B.A. and an M.A. from that institution.

After several years' experience as a teacher, vice-principal, and acting principal in three Victoria schools, Harry Gilliland returned to his first post-secondary alma mater. He was a social studies and mathematics instructor at Victoria Provincial Normal School from 1944 to 1946, when he became the School's vice-principal. In 1954, he was appointed Principal, a post he held for the final two years of normal schooling in British Columbia. With the School's absorption first into Victoria College and subsequently into the UBC system, Professor Gilliland was appointed Director of the Department of Teacher Education at the College.

Harry Gilliland was the last administrator in what could truly be called a tradition. Throughout its 40-year life, Victoria Provincial Normal School had welcomed hosts of prospective teachers from throughout Vancouver Island and the rural and remote corners of British Columbia. They had spent only months together before scattering, but uncharacteristic of many brief human contacts, they had maintained their connections. Year after year, and as recently as the 50-year reunion of the

Henry C. Gilliland, Principal, 1954 to 1956. Photo courtesy of UVic Archives, reference # 007.1107. Chapman Photography.

Class of 1951-52 in June, 2002, they returned to Victoria to renew acquaintances. Unlike the experience of people from many other institutions, this 1951-'52 class was able to hold its half-century celebration in the very gymnasium where they had exercised and played team sports during their teacher training year. To that day, the building, completely refurbished and a part of Camosun College, still contained tangible reminders of the year they had spent learning to teach. The story of the bonds that pulled these alumni and many others back to the building so many times over the years is perhaps best told by those who could say of their educational experience, "I went to Normal School."

Perhaps the building itself offers the final word. In 2003, years after a substantial restoration of the building that included resurfacing its crumbling sandstone façade, the inscription over the front entrance remained: "Normal School."

Inscription over main entrance to Victoria Provincial Normal School. Photo courtesy of Carl E. Peterson, Architect."

Notes to Chapter 4

[1] *ARPS 1913*, 29.
[2] *ARPS 1915*, A 54-55.
[3] *ARPS 1956*, p. 50.
[4] Percy Wilkinson, interview by Vernon Storey, 15 July 2002, interview 21, transcript in interviewer's file.
[5] *ARPS 1926*, pp. 53-54.
[6] *ARPS 1927*, p. 51.
[7] Ibid., p. 52.
[8] Belle C. Gibson, *Teacher-Builder: The Life and Work of J.W. Gibson* (Victoria, BC: by the author, 1961), 97.
[9] Ibid., 98.
[10] Ibid., 97.
[11] Ken Bradley, interview by Vernon Storey, 19 July 2002, interview 24, transcript in interviewer's file.
[12] Joe Lott, interview by Vernon Storey, 17 November 2002, interview 25, transcript in interviewer's file.
[13] John Jackson, interview by Vernon Storey, 17 November 2002, interview 6, transcript in interviewer's file.
[14] Joe Lott 2002.
[15] Marjorie (Thatcher) King, interview by Vernon Storey, 22 April 2003, interview 20 transcript in interviewer's file.
[16] Pat Floyd, interview by Vernon Storey, 9 August 2002, interview 14, transcript in interviewer's file.
[17] Joe Lott 2002.
[18] Ibid.
[19] Norma (Matthews) Mickelson, interview by Vernon Storey, 14 November 2002, interview 8, transcript in interviewer's file.
[20] Ibid.
[21] Ibid.
[22] Lucille Hamilton. Personal diary March 6, 1942. BCA MS 2573, 66.

23 Ibid., March 13, 1942, 73.
24 Ibid., March 7, 1942, 67.
25 Ibid., March 9, 1942, 69.
26 Diocese of British Columbia (hereinafter ADBC), "Minutes of the Executive Committee Meeting May 26, 1942" (Victoria BC: ADBC, Box 22, T63).
27 Ibid.
28 Ibid.
29 Church Committee, Parish of Christ Church Cathedral, "Minutes, Church Committee, May 12, 1942" (Victoria BC: ADBC, T464, Box 1).
30 Fred Blankenbach, to Synod solicitors, 25 July 1942, ADBC Box 22, item T63.
31 Untitled, ADBC Box 22, Item T63.
32 John Robertson 2002.
33 Ibid.
34 Ibid.
35 Dorothy (Millner) Robertson, interview with Vernon Storey 17 July 2002, interview 23f, transcript in interviewer's file.
36 Jim Whyte 2002.
37 Ibid.
38 Ibid.
39 Minutes of Senate, University of British Columbia, August, 1954.
40 Bill Cross 2002.
41 Anne (Daser) Walters, interview by Vernon Storey, 12 November 2002, interview 26, transcript in interviewer's file.
42 John Jackson 2002.
43 Harry Gilliland, "Staff Duties" (Victoria BC: University of Victoria Archives AR 329, 2.7).
44 *ARPS 1956*, 50.
45 D.L. MacLaurin, "The history of education in the Crown Colonies of Vancouver Island and British Columbia and in the Province of British Columbia" (Ph.D. diss., University of Washington, 1934), 297.

46 Joe Lott 2002
47 Marjorie (Thatcher) King 2003.
48 Norma (Matthews) Mickelson 2002.
49 Dr. Mary Harker, interview by Vernon Storey, 12 March 2003, interview 27, transcript in interviewer's file.
50 *Daily Colonist*, March 30, 1961, 5.
51 *Victoria Daily Times*, February 24, 1936.
52 Ibid., 13.
53 Ibid., February 28, 1936, 9.
54 Ibid., February 15, 1939, 6.
55 H. O. English to Col. F. T. Fairey, 12 March, 1946, University of Victoria Archives and Special Collections (hereinafter UVICA) 1980-056.
56 Ibid.
57 Ibid.
58 *Victoria Daily Times*, September 19, 1946.
59 Ibid., October 9, 1946.
60 Ibid., October 8, 1946.
61 Ibid.
62 Ibid., October 10, 1946.
63 Ibid., October 16, 1946.
64 Frank Gower, "History of the Young Building," interview recorded on videotape (1985, Victoria, BC: Camosun College), LE5V5H5.
65 Bill Cross 2002.
66 Ibid.
67 Pat Floyd 2002.
68 Dorothy (Millner) Robertson 2002.
69 Ibid.
70 Ibid.
71 Narrator, videotape "History of the Young Building" (1985, Victoria, BC: Camosun College), LE5V5H5.
72 _____, *Victoria College Development: Historical Outline*, retrieved 5 June 2002 from http://collections.ic.gc.ca/uvic///vic-col/history.html

LEARNING TO TEACH

TEACHER PREPARATION
IN VICTORIA, BC
1903-1963

Chapter 5
Toward the Classroom:
Life at Normal School

The experience of a year at Normal School represented for many British Columbia students the first formal step on the path to fulfilling their long-held dream of becoming a teacher. For others it simply seemed like a reasonable thing to do as they contemplated moving into the workforce. Most had attended small rural schools; for some this new city adventure was a major change and an adjustment in lives that to date had been quite settled and familiar. For a few, enrolling in Normal School was almost a chance occurrence, a direction-setting decision that perhaps was unclear as to its origin but that in retrospect appeared to have been a sound choice.

For some students, the decision to become a teacher seemed almost to be a fulfilment of their destiny. They had known, or at least they had sensed, that the choice of teaching as a profession held a great deal of attraction, for some almost a calling. Their stories varied widely, but for many of the Normal School students, there really was no viable second choice. Marjorie (Thatcher) King (VPNS 1940-41) drew her example from one of her own teachers:

Well, when I was a little kid I had a very special teacher, when I was in grade 1. And that was when I decided I'd like to be a teacher because she was such a special person, I thought . . . I didn't ever deviate. That was always my plan, and I was probably involved in everything there was to be involved in, in South Wellington. Went to Sunday School, and taught Sunday School, CGIT, played badminton – anything that was going I was in.[1]

Travelling by school bus was a fact of life for many rural children. For some, the daily journeys lasted the full twelve years of their public school experience. The school day began and ended on the bus, and for Anne (Daser) Walters (VPNS 1951-52), the ride was a source of inspiration. The relationship she developed with her younger fellow riders nurtured what would eventually become a career-long love for her work as a primary teacher. She finished her teaching experience not far from her childhood home, having worked with class after class of children who, like her, understood both the joys and the challenges of rural living:

> In my high school year, you know, we rode the school bus from Kersley into Quesnel, and I found that I just really loved young children, because there were lots of little kids on the bus, too, and they seemed to really come to me, "Oh, come sit with me," you know, and I thought that I would like to work with children.[2]

Not all decisions to become a teacher were the result of childhood dreams or experiences. In reality, many young people then, as today, faced the dilemma produced by those some years their senior who asked what they planned to do and when they would start their move toward productivity. Probably countless numbers have shared the angst of young Norma (Matthews) Mickelson, who built a distinguished career as a teacher and a university professor, and who eventually became the Chancellor of the University of Victoria. Norma's life-directed decision to become a teacher seemed on the face of it, simply a product of youthful spontaneity and pragmatism:

> When I finished high school, I thought, "I've got to get out of the house." I thought, "I'll go into nursing." And the counsellor at the high school . . . sent four of us down to St. Joseph's Hospital, to Mother Superior. I'm not a Catholic, but she sent us there. And a very wise woman – that woman took us through that hospital, through every part of it, bedpans, and operating rooms, and, the smell . . . I can still remember standing at the corner of Yates and Douglas, waiting for the light and saying, "What can I do?" I knew I didn't want to work at Kresge's for the rest of my life, "What can I do quickly to get into the workforce." And the answer was, "Teaching - one year." That's why I went to Normal School.[3]

Over the years, practicalities were as important as pragmatics for these students. Most came from modest backgrounds. Many were the children of European immigrants who had moved to the land of promise to make a better life for their offspring. They had worked on the railroads and in the mines, determined that things would be better for the next generation. These young people had grown up with an understanding of tough times and a clearly conveyed sense of responsibility:

> *Remember, we were the Depression/wartime generation. And so, from the Depression we learned, you'd better bloody well get a job or you can starve to death. And from the war, you learned that you could be killed. And so, I think that the attitude was good, we're into a place that's going to get us into a job for life.*

> *And I think in the main, most people appreciated most of the Normal School stuff, except being treated like we were much younger than we were quite often. But some of the people at Normal School were only 16 or 17. A number of us were in our twenties . . . most of us had a work background of some kind. I'd been to sea, and I'd been commercial fishing. When I was at Normal School I delivered ice for Wilson's Ice at the same time.[4]*

These young people knew the sacrifices their parents had made to send them not only to school, but far away to school, out of touch with family and friends and far from homes where they could live without encountering the costs they would experience when they moved to the city.

Counting the Cost

It was all new, some of it expected and some unanticipated – bus fares, tuition fees, room and board, everyday expenses. There were no dormitories at the Normal School. A list of available boarding places was posted, and for many, an early task on arriving in town was to find a place to live. Some of those living places were hospitable second homes; others were the cheerless, unwelcoming premises of people who simply saw an opportunity to augment their income by taking in a boarder or two. In many cases, fair exchange and mutual assistance were important currencies:

You'd hardly believe, my father had to mortgage the farm to raise $120 to pay my tuition. And then I worked for my board. And my mother gave me $5.00 a month for spending money . . . And I know that I broke my glasses while I was there, and the man where I was staying had a business here . . . he said if I would come down and wash the floor in his office, he would pay me $5.00 to get my glasses repaired. Things were pretty slim.[5]

Marjorie (Thatcher) King scrubbing floors to pay for glasses repair. Photo courtesy of Marjorie King.

Earlier, I noted Principal Harry English's program of assisting students whose finances were not sufficient to outfit them for life at school in the city. Some, in fact, had barely enough to get by:

One of the girls came from Prince George and she had one dress and one pair of shoes. So she didn't go to the parties because she was ashamed to be seen in . . . the same dress that she went to school in. She washed it every couple of days, and she only had two sets of underwear, and one pair of stockings.[6]

For all, there were adjustments. For some, the pressures were primarily financial. Many found support and camaraderie in this small group of peers who had been thrown together in their pursuit of a common dream – to become a teacher. As Anne (Daser) Walters said during our conversation, "I guess we just leaned on each other."[7]

Adjusting to City Life

For students coming to Victoria from rural British Columbia, some on their first trip away from home, this was a weighty adventure. The young capital city, which had been incorporated for just over 50 years, was for many a vastly different scene from the rural settings of their childhood and youth. That change of scene was not only a reality for students enrolling in the very early years; it met their successors 20 and 30 years later. John Jackson recalled his creative effort to ensure he would not get lost in the big city in 1943:

I was a country boy. And every street I went by I made a note of it, so I'd know my way back. I was definitely country and more than country, I'd never been to school up until Grade 9 (I was taught at home), and I was three years older than I should be at that grade [because of health].[8]

Even as late as 1951, just a few years before the Province's Normal Schools would be closed in favour of university-based programs of teacher education, moving to Victoria was for many a major adjustment. They were moving not only to different surroundings but also to a new and unfamiliar social setting. Anne (Daser) Walters, an alumnus from that year, recalled her first days at Normal School as a teenaged girl from a tiny Cariboo community:

Oh, it was just, it was just such a big adjustment for this country kid, you know, and I felt it was me. I was very insecure, I had no self-confidence. I had lots of self-confidence in high school, but you know, I knew everything and everybody so well, and then going to this whole strange place where everybody else seemed so polished and so well-dressed and so talented and all this, it was tough, it was.

Before that summer, I had never been further than Prince George north, and Williams Lake south. And so, it was really something learning to get around, you know, just learning to use city buses. I expected the fare would be different for each place you wanted to get off, instead of just a dime all over the city. Embarrassing myself, and things like that . . . I wanted to walk as much as I could, because I was on a very tight budget. I did a lot of walking. A lot of very lonely times but I wasn't going to let my father's money spent that far go to waste.[9]

Others recalled incidents not so readily classified. What Anne recalled as an embarrassment related to a country kid's lack of social graces may in fact have been a normal and common, though unfortunate, experience of late adolescence:

> *The Social Studies teacher, now, I have to say I was very*
> *uncomfortable with him, and he actually – you know, it's*
> *funny how you remember something like that for years, but he*
> *went out of his way to embarrass me one morning . . . if the*
> *same thing happened now, I would laugh it off. But, at that*
> *time, it just, it really threw me.[10]*

But they survived. With the passage of time, life's hurdles and embarrassments softened and warmed into the cherished memories that these teachers were happy to share with others, and especially with those who had shared the experience.

New Living Arrangements

Many of the Normal School students had lived at home with their parents until moving to Victoria for teacher training. The familiarity of a country home and close companions was exchanged for the reality of life in a city where one now had to make decisions about the basic necessities of life. As I noted above, that included finding accommodation in an unfamiliar community. Alumnus Percy Wilkinson (VPNS 1926-27) recalled the process:

> *Of course, there were no residences. A lot of people around the*
> *Normal School had their names and addresses in at the*
> *Normal School office, so that when people applied from*
> *Kelowna or Timbuktu or wherever, and indicated that they*
> *would like to have some names and addresses of residences*
> *nearby, they were able to provide them. Many of them lived, in*
> *fact most of them lived, within walking distance. Most of us*
> *were quite prepared to walk up to two miles two ways. In*
> *those days . . . everybody walked.[11]*

Walking distance, clearly, was not a major problem. Most boarding places were located in fairly close proximity to the Normal School. There were other problems, though, and not all of their stories had happy endings:

> *You know, they supplied us with a list of board places and*
> *work-for-board places, and I went to a place that I was to*
> *work for my board, and it was just "pick a name out of a hat,"*
> *and it was an unhappy situation. I lasted, I think, a little over*

a week, and then, these people that I knew in Victoria, or had known as a child, I just sort of landed on their doorstep in tears. I think I phoned first, and I did stay with them the rest of the year.[12]

There were other inconveniences, many of them simply a part of life's normal occurrences. Understandably, some landlords became concerned at any suggestion that their family's health could be compromised by their boarder. One wonders, though, whether the action taken in one instance was too little, too late:

My big problem was that I got measles in the middle of the term. And the people where I was staying had three children. They didn't think I should be there. So, I had an aging aunt and uncle who lived in Victoria, and I went and stayed with them while I got rid of my measles. German measles, which was a bit of a nuisance. But the people were very kind to me.[13]

Home for the Holidays

For students from the Interior of the province, travelling home for the Christmas break was an adventure, especially in the early years. A former student recalled being offered, with her girlfriend, a ride from the coast to the southern Okanagan in December. The two young men had a car, but there was a problem. The vehicle was a coupe with a rumble seat. The boys had been chivalrous enough to offer the two young women a ride, but apparently that was where consideration ended. The men rode inside the car, the women under a stiff tarpaulin in the rumble seat! It was not explained how the girls made the return trip, or whether the icy relationships ever thawed.

The first leg of the trip from Victoria, of course, involved travel by boat to Vancouver. From there the journey was typically by train to and from the Okanagan, if that was where one lived. The pressure was off in December of 1943 for John Jackson and his fellow students on their way home for a break, and their trip was marked by exuberance and improvisation:

And I remember on one occasion . . . on the train. On the way home at Christmas, some chaps from the university had, I guess, celebrated. And going up at that long incline at the Coquihalla, they got out behind the train and there was the thought of pushing. And the poor conductor, of course, was driving himself wild, because if they had ever been left behind, they would have been stiff the next morning. The Coquihalla, of course, was a tremendous, marvellous journey.

We took the seats...and turned them around so there were seats facing inwards. We put the tops of the seats as benches, and two people slept between the two chairs turned around. It was a very enjoyable journey, the snow...And oh yes, it took about – let me see now. You'd leave here by boat, and catch the train in Vancouver, and arrive in the afternoon, I guess. But, travel all night. But that would be the Coquihalla railway.[14]

Once back in Victoria, the students faced the second half of their nine-month program. They had experienced a limited amount of time in the schools, primarily to observe, and now they would prepare for practica and completion of their courses. Not all was work, though – they found time for a variety of social and recreational activities.

A Social Life

Downtown Victoria was an inviting place during the war. Beyond having the Normal School, this was a college town and a major naval installation. The names of establishments, and perhaps the choice of activities, have changed over the years, but perennially, there have been places to gather and congenial companions with whom to gather. Jim Whyte (VPNS 1945-46), who enrolled in the Normal school after returning from military service, recalled:

Terry's Cafe on the corner of [Fort] and Douglas was a big spot...a wonderful cafe. And you could get sandwiches and all that sort of stuff. A lot of the people gathered there. And there was another place up on Yates, called Wimpy's, which was a hamburger joint – we used to go there. The only soldiers I remember very much were on, I think they called it, Gus' Corner, which I think was Yates and Douglas . . . And the soldiers and sailors picked up their bus at the corner, there was a Cunningham Drug Store, and drove out to Esquimalt.[15]

There were also Normal School social activities, although the male-female balance offered its own challenges. Marjorie

(Thatcher) King recalled circumstances that from her perspective were quite acceptable:

> *Well, there were only ten boys in the class, and there were about 80 girls, so they had to bring in some fellows from someplace else. And I don't remember any particular arrangements being made. I always seemed to have somebody to go with, so I don't remember.*[16]

Marjorie was short on funds, had to work for her board, and had limited time to socialize, but she recalled some occasions with delight:

> *I remember doing a Spanish Waltz at a party that we had. There were eight of us chosen to do this Spanish Waltz, and I got to be one of them. And I was the youngest of the whole class, so I felt quite honoured. And then I know that we had some social events with the College...the person I went with brought me a gardenia . . . beautiful. And I remember standing at the top of the stairs at the Craigdarroch, looking over the edge, and I remember thinking, "Now, that's what a fairy princess feels like." . . . I have happy memories of my time there. I didn't have much time for social life because I was working for my room and board. They had three children that I looked after, and then I had homework to do, and I had no money . . . But I participated in everything.*[17]

Some activities were organized by the students themselves, and in some instances they also provided the music:

> *There were activities, yes, a number of activities including dances that we held during the year. We had our own dance band. A lot of the fellows were very good musicians, and they formed an excellent dance band. I wasn't myself, but we had a choir which I sang in, we did a number of concerts. And . . . we had a lot of partying together. And then, within the class, there would be subgroups, so I had a group of four or five fellows, all from the Interior, who I chummed around with. And two of us happened to be opera nuts, so that was sort of what stuck us together.*[18]

There was sometimes a curious mismatch between the regular reminders by faculty members to these students that they were young men and women about to assume full adult roles in the community, and a parallel assumption that they were far from ready to take on the tasks of adulthood. Marjorie (Thatcher) King was prepared to take on the challenge:

> *We had a budget for our social affairs at the Normal School, and I seemed to have been on the Social Committee, I guess, because I remember we had some kind of a ruling that we couldn't do this and we couldn't do that, and whatever, and so on and so forth. And I remember going to Dr. [sic] Denton, sassy thing that I was, I said to him, "Dr. Denton, if we're expected to go out and teach a class in the boondocks and manage the whole thing, how is it that you don't think that we're able to handle $10 here for our social affairs." And he looked at me, and he said, 'You have a point, Miss Thatcher." And he gave it to us.[19]*

Not all activities were officially sanctioned, and some that were, continued unofficially long after chaperones and instructors had departed. Pat Floyd (VPNS 1955-56) recalled a memorable celebration:

> *And we had a famous blowout at the end of the year. We had a picnic, an officially arranged picnic at Willows, and I can't quite recall if the party ended up on the beach at Willows, or some of us went to Cadboro Bay. And I think we drank too much. What happened was that someone had discovered there was a pot of money left in one of the Social funds, so after the faculty members of the Normal School had gone home, and half the Normal School class had disappeared, the rest of us stayed on the beach. And one of the fellows went to get the money. I guess he was old enough to get in the Liquor Store. He came back with I don't know how many cases of beer, all of which got consumed. And then we lined the beer bottles up along the beach afterwards, it was a long line of empty beer bottles. So, that was the finale of Normal School.[20]*

His closing comment was a telling one, given that this was the end not only of the 1955-56 school year, but also of the Victoria Provincial Normal School's life. After that, all get-togethers would need to be in the form of class reunions. Despite the minor mischief reported by some of our interviewees, all were clear about the expectations awaiting them as they moved out into the world of teaching – they eyes of the community would be pointed in their direction, fully expecting that as Normal School graduates they would be icons of respectability in their communities.

Very Respectable Persons

Throughout the Victoria Provincial Normal School years, some remarkable constants prevailed in the schools of Canada's far western province. Though British Columbia was both far from Great Britain and Europe geographically and by the early 20th century increasingly distant in time from the Victorian era, some norms held fast. Through two world wars, the Great Depression, and the passage of 40 years' time, the message to Normal School students was clear and constant. They were to be teachers, and with that came a high level of responsibility to be both good citizens and examples to others in the community, especially children. In 1939, candidacy included two specific non-academic requirements that probably would not have been acceptable some years later: "Applicants . . . must present a certificate of good moral character . . . must be free from obvious language and speech defects."[21]

The comments of one young about-to-be teacher just five years before the Normal School was to close could as easily have been made by a fellow traveller from the 1920s. Asked whether certain expectations still held in the latter years, Anne (Daser) Walters responded:

> *Oh, yes, my goodness. You must not wear a kerchief, you must wear a hat. You must certainly never be seen in a place where alcohol was served. You must not be seen at the school wearing slacks. If it was really so cold that you had to go to school in slacks, you had to change before the kids got there (in the outdoor toilet, so as not to be caught). And, of course, just be this very respectable person.*[22]

A student enrolled ten years earlier noted, "There was an unwritten dress code. For example, we often wore suits and shirts and ties."[23] The message persisted throughout the lifetime of the Normal School. Alumnus Percy Wilkinson (1926-27) born in Oregon and raised in the United States and Canada, had understood the rules early and very clearly. Even though (or perhaps because) he was a few years older than his compatriots, he was certainly informed of the essentials of a soon-to-be teacher's decorum in the 1926-27 Normal School year:

> *In those days, of course, we were most careful. You didn't smoke, and you didn't drink. If you went to public dances,*

Students on a bench under a tree outside the Normal School building, ca 1950.
Photo courtesy of UVic Archives, reference # 007.1833.

*well, if you danced in a sedate way, it was all right, but if it
was anything out of the ordinary, it would get back. Nothing
out of the ordinary, the straight and narrow. Seeking the right
company was important, and we were told various streets in
Victoria were not* a propos.[24]

The comments of interviewees were remarkably consistent,
borne in messages conveyed by instructors most of whom, albeit
years earlier, had taught in the public schools themselves. Dress,
behaviour, associates, and appropriate settings for social activities
– all were listed, prescribed, and passed on to these young people.
Most of them had arrived at their teacher training year towards
the end of their own adolescence. Many had come from more rural
and sheltered settings; all quickly gained a keen awareness that
they were standing at the brink of a very public life. Norma
(Matthews) Mickelson remembered the instructions clearly:

*Oh, absolutely, you had to hold up the torch, you were a
teacher. And you were expected to dress like a teacher should,
and act like a teacher should. I can remember, and I don't
know where this came from, but I can still remember the
advice that you just did not be seen in public in a beer parlour.
You were a teacher, and you didn't. And this business of going
down on Friday afternoon for a beer after work, no, no. It was
a no-no. We had a lot of stuff on deportment, and how to act,
and how to behave.[25]*

The Victoria Provincial Normal School student population was
drawn largely from 'small town British Columbia.' That group
differed markedly from those attending the Vancouver Provincial
Normal School, who had been drawn from Vancouver and its
immediate surroundings. To a considerable extent, those
regularities have persisted, though the reality is changing
markedly with the advent of community colleges and university
colleges. The Victoria students knew that even if they did not
return to their home areas, and many did, they would probably
spend at least a portion of their careers in small rural schools and
communities. In those settings, they were told, they would be
visible and observed:

*The message was to really keep your nose clean, because most
of us were going to go and teach in small communities, where
we would be very noticeable. And many of us came, a good
portion of the class came from the Interior . . . Certainly, not
drinking. I kind of remember smoking being mentioned – I
didn't smoke, I guess that's why I didn't pay attention to any
comments they made about smoking, I never smoked,
anyway, so it didn't really matter to me. But certainly,
alcohol, and the women, of course. [It was] implied that they
should be very careful about their behaviour.[26]*

The experience base of the Normal School instructors, their
admonitions from their years 'in the trenches,' contributed to a
collective feeling among the students that they were engaged in a
noble pursuit that was not for everyone. The standards were clear
and high, and Normal School professors often considered
themselves responsible to stand *in loco parentis* to monitor the
activities of those who had arrived for this year of initiation:

*I think that there always a subtle feeling that you should be of
good moral character. I certainly am aware of people being*

pulled aside and talked to about their activities off-campus. So, that was part of it. But the whole thing…the real enterprise was getting you ready to teach in the coming year. Very practical, and you felt very confident because everybody that was teaching you had taught in the schools of British Columbia. And, indeed, some of them were sort of a central elite of the teachers of British Columbia. It was a bit of an old boys' club. Expectations both ways.[27]

Some interviewees recalled personal admonitions passed on by their instructors just before the graduates left to assume their teaching positions. Some of the messages were conveyed specifically to young women:

I remember one of our instructors, Dr. Anderson, just before we finished and went out into the world, her advice to us was, "Do not marry the first man you meet in Skunk Hollow!" That was her advice.[28]

The scrutiny did not stop with the end of the Normal School year. In some instances the message initially delivered by parent-like instructors during the pre-service year was verified and reinforced by an employer. Jim Whyte recalled:

I know a lady I taught with, and it was in the 1930s, and she was sitting on the beach with her boyfriend, and she was having a cigarette. Somebody from the School Board saw her and she was hauled in, and told, "Any of that ruddy behaviour, and you're out."[29]

The debate about whether schools should lead or follow society's norms, needs, and expectations has been both perennial and largely unresolved. It was made clear, though, to these Normal School students that as teachers, their moral leadership would be evidenced by their social followership, even in matters such as dress: "It was a long time before you didn't wear a shirt and a tie, and a jacket, even a sport jacket was a bit risqué."[30]

Approaching his 100th birthday in 2003, Percy Wilkinson (VPNS 1926-27) still recalled that the world awaiting him and his newly certified colleagues was not entirely certain. He was clear, though, about his goal, which he may well have achieved at a level higher than he credited himself:

I didn't have much idea as to what was ahead of me. I hoped that I would somehow learn how to be a super teacher, which

I never did become. However, I did enjoy my year at Normal School. I think probably because I was older than most; there were one or two older than me, the average age of the girls was about 17 to 20, and the boys were about 18 to about 21 or 22.[31]

The feeling was frequently expressed, and those memories have been affirmed at many class reunions, that the Normal School year was generally an enjoyable experience. The students knew well the culture of the day and the particular expectations they faced as prospective teachers. They also lived the lives of adventurous young people, they recalled in interviews. With a certain degree of risk, there were ways to pursue a variety of sometimes mildly rebellious activities. Marjorie (Thatcher) King recalled her adventure with makeup:

I remember we weren't supposed to wear lipstick or do anything like that. And most of us didn't anyway – most of us didn't have the money for it and we hadn't been brought up [to use it], I don't know, we just weren't. And I remember a friend and I decided that, we were going to have some. I remember we went out, and she bought some lipstick (I didn't have any money), then we shared it when we went out somewhere, I don't know where we went. But we sure didn't wear it to school . . . our deportment was to be above reproach.[32]

Some of the boundaries around social relations also reflected the expectation of decorum. Marjorie recalled the cost of overstepping limits that sometimes seemed of unclear origin and relevance:

We were being instructed to be very proper, you know, and there were two students who came from the same town, and knew each other before they came here. And they happened to be out walking on a Sunday afternoon, and Mr. Gough came along and took them home because that was a no-no . . . We weren't supposed to consort with each other, I guess. I don't know why not . . . because some of us did, we just didn't get caught.[33]

Typical of the day, perhaps, accounts of actual "highjinks" mostly were reported by male members of the Normal School classes. Mr. Dudley Wickett, the School's music instructor during the 1940s and an individual many years these students' senior, was a focus of both friendly recollection and adolescent playfulness:

> *Mr. Wickett was the Music teacher, and some of the boys, I don't know who, had got into the piano and rigged it up with hair pins or something. So, he'd be playing along and all of a sudden, it goes "sproinnng!" And we always sang. He always wanted to sing Old Black Joe, and we sang Old Jack Blow.[34]*

These students were not the original inventors of mischief. The Normal School building was adorned on top by a clock tower visible from a great distance that afforded, for those brave enough to risk being caught, a commanding view of the city. Joe Lott was enrolled at the Normal School during 1941-42, just before the building was taken over for use as a military hospital. He recalled his own foray into forbidden territory:

> *We horsed around. One day, for example, Alec and I got up into the clock tower which, of course, was completely verboten, but we were really just kids, that's all, at 18 years of age. And we explored the clock tower and looked out over the city from up there. Didn't get caught, so it was an experience.[35]*

Some misdemeanours that seemed relatively trivial to the students represented important teaching opportunities to their instructors and to Normal School officials. Clearly, the students were expected to be exemplars of responsibility at all times. However, as Norma (Matthews) Mickelson observed, events that occurred around the world and shaped the history of humanity were secondary in importance to the observance of Normal School protocols, at least in the mind of one administrator:

> *I was at Normal School when VE Day occurred. We didn't go to school...And I can remember coming back the next morning . . . the principal had marked the students who hadn't shown up, and the students who had shown up, and the students who were late. And up in the front of the auditorium, he read out a certain number of names. These were the people who showed up on time, and another certain number of names, these were the people who showed up late, and another certain number of names, these were the people who didn't even come. And then we had this huge lecture on reliability. It didn't matter what*

the situation was, you came on time . . . War or nothing. And I was one of the delinquents.[36]

It has been said that those who do not pay attention to history are doomed to repeat its mistakes. Many times during the interviews I heard stories about the Normal School days, some told as fond memories of models provided, some recalled as practices to avoid, many recalled with the clarity of yesterdays that remained fresh. Whatever the nature of the recall, these were the days to be remembered, the days when one learned to teach.

Notes to Chapter 5

[1] Marjorie (Thatcher) King 2003.
[2] Anne (Daser) Walters 2002.
[3] Norma (Matthews) Mickelson 2002.
[4] Bill Cross 2002.
[5] Marjorie (Thatcher) King 2003.
[6] Marjorie (Campbell) Brown, interview by Vernon Storey, 5 November 2002, interview 11, transcript in interviewer's file.
[7] Anne (Daser) Walters 2002.
[8] John Jackson 2002.
[9] Anne (Daser) Walters 2002.
[10] Ibid.
[11] Percy Wilkinson 2002.
[12] Anne (Daser) Walters 2002.
[13] Marjorie (Thatcher) King 2003.
[14] John Jackson 2002.
[15] Jim Whyte 2002.
[16] Marjorie (Thatcher) King 2003.
[17] Ibid.
[18] Pat Floyd 2002.
[19] Marjorie (Thatcher) King 2003.
[20] Pat Floyd 2002.
[21] Department of Education, *Regulations and Courses of Study for Provincial Normal Schools* (Victoria: Department of Education, 1939).
[22] Anne (Daser) Walters 2002.
[23] Joe Lott 2002.
[24] Percy Wilkinson 2002.
[25] Norma (Matthews) Mickelson 2002.
[26] Pat Floyd 2002.
[27] Bill Cross 2002.
[28] Norma (Matthews) Mickelson 2002.
[29] Jim Whyte 2002.
[30] John Robertson 2002.
[31] Percy Wilkinson 2002.
[32] Marjorie (Thatcher) King 2003.
[33] Ibid.
[34] Jim Whyte 2002.
[35] Joe Lott 2002.
[36] Norma (Matthews) Mickelson 2002.

LEARNING TO TEACH

TEACHER PREPARATION
IN VICTORIA, BC
1903-1963

Chapter 6
Learning and Practising

Prevailing perspectives of the normal school period on what was involved in becoming an elementary school teacher were reflected in a government news report published just prior to the closure of these two British Columbia institutions:

In general, the type of training given in these schools consisted mainly of a review of the elementary-school curriculum, with the addition of studies of educational psychology, principles of teaching, and special methods of teaching the various subjects, together with opportunities for practice teaching.[1]

Since the early years of schooling in the province, there had been a clear difference between the preparation path of elementary teachers and that of their high school colleagues. The latter was clearly regarded as a task of the university, a sentiment captured by Putman and Weir in their 1925 survey report. The Commissioners observed:

The Province of British Columbia has taken the advanced position that high school teachers must be university graduates. More than this, these graduates must have a full year of professional training after receiving the Bachelor's degree in Arts or Science before being given a licence [sic] to teach. This is a commendable requirement and one fully justified by the importance of the high school as a means of general culture and as a preparatory school for the University.[2]

In contrast with the 35 pages of text and 15 recommendations focusing on the preparation of elementary school teachers, the

Commissioners' treatment of secondary teacher preparation amounted to four pages of text. Their three related recommendations dealt with the hiring of a professor, discussions around the possibility of a university-affiliated public school, and the endorsement of secondary teachers' certificates noting subject areas of qualification. That passing consideration was preceded by the statement that:

> The Survey Commission has no mandate to make any investigation into the work of the University. But as the University, through an arrangement with the Department of Education, has undertaken the preparation of high school teachers, and as this professional training is closely related to the efficiency of the high schools, the Survey deems it proper to say something of this one phase of University work.[3]

Thus Putman and Weir distanced themselves from any critical examination of the work of preparing high school teachers. Perhaps not yet satisfied that they had made their point, and apparently anxious to have clean investigative hands, the Commissioners hinted at the potential for conflict of interest as their rationale for standing at a distance. One of them had worked in the University's secondary teacher preparation program for a term, and his duties had been assumed by temporary instructors during his absence. With those caveats in view, the pair noted:

> The Survey has made little attempt critically to examine the instruction now being given in the University [of British Columbia] School of Education...our remarks must be confined to a consideration of the general plan of organization and its future possibilities.[4]

As noted previously, the Normal Schools were afforded no such consideration. The tone of the report's chapter on the Normal Schools was captured in a single terse paragraph:

> We trust that the deficiencies we have noted have not blinded us to the many good features of the work we have seen. If we seem to make more of defects than of strong points it is not because we are incapable of noting what is meritorious but because defects must be pointed out and even emphasized before they can be removed.[5]

Over time, some intra-group distinctions within organizations are absorbed into their prevailing culture. That has been the case, though it has diminished in recent years, in regard to what might be termed an elementary/secondary distinction within the teaching profession. The teachers who are the focus of this book were instructed under a clear mandate – they were being prepared to teach in elementary schools. Yet in practice, the lines have often been blurred. Many of those teachers taught secondary grades and subjects during their careers. Many teachers in rural schools taught all who arrived to be schooled, regardless of their age or grade.

As candidates for the profession, these young people were clear about their goal – to become teachers. Their journeys, both before and after Normal School, varied immensely. They formed strong friendships with their fellow students very quickly, because they would have little time together before embarking on their careers. Many recall those days with great clarity and freshness. This book, in the next two chapters particularly, attempts to preserve their stories and weave them into a larger tapestry that will display something of the adventure.

Training for Teaching

Our terminology has shifted over the history of schooling in British Columbia. Typically we refer now to programs of teacher *education*, speaking of pre-service *preparation* as we describe the process of gaining qualifications and moving toward certification. Gradually, we have abandoned the term teacher *training* as evidence of a previous era in the development of the craft. Clearly, though, the enterprise in which North America's normal schools were engaged for many years was that of teacher *training*.

A comment made frequently by interviewees for this project was that at the Victoria Provincial Normal School, they had learned how to teach. There was a clear focus in the Normal Schools on a basic, school curriculum-focused program that included much emphasis on classroom routines and regularities. In terms that might have gladdened the heart of Frederick W. Taylor and other proponents of scientific management, many instructors were concerned with imparting to their students the 'one best way' to do teaching.

More than one Normal School graduate referred to the long-remembered practice of a particular instructor's demonstration of how one should display a picture or other exhibit by moving around the classroom to designated positions. Doing this, he stated, would ensure that everyone had a clear view of the item. The students took some of these admonishments 'with a grain of salt.' One class assembled an album of generally friendly caricatures and poems to describe various attributes and practices of their instructors. A page was devoted to the "Seven Positions" touted by this instructor as the one best way to display visual aids.

Some 'best way' admonitions continued virtually unchanged throughout the Normal School's history. Not all of them were focused on matters at the heart of teaching. Pat Floyd graduated in 1956, the School's final year of operation. He recalled the preoccupation of one instructor with the "one best way" to clean a blackboard:

> I do remember . . . that you had to know how to clean a blackboard. We had many demonstrations on how to clean a blackboard . . . Well, it was up and down, and then when you've done all the board up and down and got it clean, then you go across the top and the bottom, horizontally. So you do all these vertical strokes, and then two horizontal strokes to finish off the job. And, that was about all I remember from that class, really.[6]

The interviewees conveyed both a general warmth for the Normal School and its instructors, and in some cases a realization of its shortcomings. Pat Floyd recalled "the close relationship you developed with faculty . . . really more of a teacher-student relationship than a professor-student relationship . . . these were mostly all former teachers themselves . . . there was a whole raft of them."[7] Marjorie (Thatcher) King recalled specific memorable interactions with some of the people who introduced her to the world of the classroom during her Normal School year:

> I remember Dr. Anderson was an instructor, and I remember her saying (this was a period when incidental learning was being promoted) . . ."Just make sure that this incidental learning doesn't become accidental." Which I thought was kind of neat. And we had Barbara Hinton, who was the Phys Ed instructor . . . every inch a lady . . . she never seemed to have a hair out of place, and she was the loveliest person, and yet she taught us Phys Ed . . . she just seemed to float around the gym.[8]

Several interviewees were also clear about what the Normal School was and what it was not. Norma (Matthews) Mickelson may have captured the essence:

Normal School was not like a university program. Normal School was a methodological program, that's what it was. You learned how to teach. You might not have had much to teach, but you learned how to do it . . . In some ways, the Normal School was very, very good methodology training, but in other ways, it was really deficient. I mean, when I started to teach, it never occurred to me that those little grade one children, once they'd finished that work, could go and get library books. You were supposed to keep them busy all the time. So, in one way, it was very useful, in another way, I think there were a lot of deficiencies, too . . . Yes, I think that the Normal School was where you went to learn to be a teacher . . . to be trained, and that's what it was, and that's what you did . . . So, we really did know how to teach.[9]

Anne (Daser) Walters, a colleague from a subsequent year, recalled some eight years after Norma's experience that the connection between theory and practice was not always evident in Normal School classes:

I felt that they really fell short on what they were teaching. They talked about individual differences, but as far as really giving us the tools and the knowledge to deal with . . . every class, you end up with somebody that can't read yet, two years below their level . . . and I don't feel they prepared us at all for that, not properly. The child psychology course would have been useful a few years later, but it was hard to stay awake in them.[10]

That comment may also have reflected the observation made by some former students about another reality – that much of their preparation was based on the assumption that the teacher would be working in a single-grade classroom rather than in the multi-grade situations that would be the norm for many.

Perhaps because of the experience base of some early Normal School faculty members, there was sometimes a certain 'disconnect' between teacher training curriculum and the realities of rural multi-graded classrooms. Several interviewees commented on the classroom world that they discovered only when they left

Victoria to begin teaching. Percy Wilkinson (VPNS 1926-27) noted that:

> *The emphasis was on the timetable in a single grade room, and most of them never got to a class of that type. In other words, they had to struggle . . . how do you teach four or eight grades in one room? Obviously, you have to take three grades here, three grades there, and three grades there . . . you did the best you could.*[11]

In addition to facing the reality of multiple grades, these graduates would be required to teach the full array of subjects to their students. They recalled instructors' efforts to prepare them for the breadth of demand inherent in their teaching assignments. Their comments were anecdotal rather than systematic in most cases, offering a human glimpse into their experiences.

Across the Curriculum, Across the Grades

Throughout the Normal School's four-decade life, staff and administrators were clear about what they perceived as the School's mandate and mission. To a considerable extent, the interviewees' comments about the nature of the training experience were also timeless. Pat Floyd's comment from 1955-56, the final year of operation, seems remarkably similar to one that might have been offered by a predecessor from a much earlier year:

> *We were being trained as elementary school teachers . . . maybe one or two people had degrees, but the majority did not . . . So, we were being trained as elementary school teachers, and certainly the . . . majority of the teachers at the Normal School, were from elementary school. So, it was very broad, we really went across the full curriculum. I can't say there was any one area, other than perhaps reading, that was emphasized more than another.*[12]

It is a long-held tenet of the culture and language of elementary school teaching that the primary focus of practice is the learner. Perhaps we tend to identify that as a relatively new perspective. In fact, it has marked the history of public education in this province, including the history of instruction at the Normal School, since the early days. Norma (Matthews) Mickelson, who

Male students in class at Victoria Provincial Normal School in 1947-48. Photo courtesy of UVic Archives, reference # 006.1005.

attended classes in Memorial Hall during the Second World War, recalled:

> There was no course in Child Psychology. But we had . . . our primary teacher, primary instructor, and she was very good at talking about the fact that you're not teaching subjects in the primary grades, you're teaching children.[13]

The message these students understood was that through the Normal School experience, one learned how to teach. If that was true, then it was reasonable to expect that their skills would be adaptable to a variety of situations:

> I remember years later when I was substituting, after I was married and had children and so on, I was asked to teach. We lived in the Interior, and I was asked to go into the high school and teach. Glory be! it was The Rise and Fall of the Third Reich! That was the subject I was asked to take for the teacher who was having an operation . . . grade 10, I think it was. And I remember saying, "But I'm not a high school teacher, that's not my field, you know." And I remember him, the principal, saying to me, "But you know how to teach." So, then I had to learn The Rise and Fall of the Third Reich. But that was the message . . . we were taught how to teach.[14]

The business of learning how to teach was practiced from the beginning of the Normal School year. Each class was treated as an actual elementary school class; the teachers in training as pupils in that class. Interviewees recalled very clearly the performance dimension of their work, particularly in regard to music and speech. Regularly, the classes would prepare and present programs to their colleagues:

> *And the Normal School prepared you for a number of things. Every Monday we held an assembly, just as you would in schools, in those days. Each class had responsibility for the assembly each week, a different class . . . You were supposed to put on plays and musical things, and you'd recruit from one another's classrooms - men would recruit women, or women men, when they needed that in what they were doing. There was also a Christmas Concert that you had to put on, good practice for putting on a Christmas Concert when you hit school. And a lot of singing. A very large choir developed, and went around singing at various venues, and things like that.[15]*

The focus of these performance activities was on practising the skills that the classroom would demand. Students drew on their own skills and experiences, where possible, to participate with their colleagues in weekly assemblies of the student body. These events were not only informational for the participants in this era before electronic communication systems, they were instructional:

VPNS Spring Concert Players, 1948
Photo courtesy of UVic Archives, reference # 007.1602. Bill Halkett photographer.

Theatre production of "Homework," Dorothy (Millner) Robertson waving in background, Class X, 1945-46. Photo courtesy of UVic Archives, reference # 006.1208.

You put on an entertainment, or a talk, or something for the whole ruddy bunch of them. And I remember, I was very fond of the Warsaw Concerto at that time, and I played the Warsaw Concerto, and we talked about it.[16]

Students did not necessarily arrive at Normal School with the well-developed skills in public speaking or music teaching. Many recalled their experiences during the process of being taught how to do both. Spontaneity was sometimes the requirement, presumably as preparation to think quickly on one's feet, and "When it was your turn, she'd give you a topic, and you had to speak on it, extemporaneously."[17] Several interviewees recalled their experiences with an activity that at first intimidated many:

We had a speech instructor who was a wonderful woman, and I can remember her standing in front of us and saying, "Breathe." And some of the students, when we had to do a little speech, they'd be too nervous, and I can remember her saying, "You've nothing to be nervous about, nervousness is a form of conceit. You're thinking about yourself. Stop thinking about yourself. And, straighten the seams in your stockings and comb your hair before you leave home, and then concentrate on your subject, and you'll have no problem."[18]

Mrs. Reese-Burns, the elocution instructor, appears to have had an understanding not only of technique, but also of students' needs to develop the self-confidence they would require in managing their own classes. Joe Lott, for one, appreciated her skill:

> *Mrs. Reese-Burns, who taught speech and public speaking . . . did me a very good turn, because I was kind of a bashful kid. And she would just put you up on the stage and give you a slip of paper and say, "Talk on that for two or three minutes." And you had to. It wasn't an alternative. You didn't say, to hell with you, like some kids might say today. You did it. And after a few months of that sort of thing it became easier and easier to just get up there and speak.[19]*

Mrs. Reese-Burns' style was also captured in a friendly verse written by a member of the class of 1945-46 for that group's 50th reunion:

> *And speeches were made at the drop of a hat;*
> *Extemporaneous they called it, we laughed at all that.*
> *Speak from the diaphragm, stand up tall;*
> *Enunciate clearly, throw your voice to the hall.[20]*

All of the students were required to extend their vocal skills beyond speech to singing. Many recalled fondly Mr. "Dudley" Wickett, an instructor many years their senior. Norma (Matthews) Mickelson remembered also his tireless efforts to teach his students the skills of conducting, recalling, "Now, Mr. Wickett, who was the Music teacher . . . he'd coach us in how to do the conducting and so on. We did all that – we actually did it. That was our class."[21]

Not all of Percy Wickett's students considered themselves musically talented. Marjorie (Thatcher) King remembered his efforts on behalf of those among the Normal School students who were less gifted in that area than others:

> *And then Mr. Wickett was the music teacher . . . he had the classes divided into two groups, those who had had some music and those of us who had not. And he struggled valiantly with those of us who were not musical, to teach us to sing the Ash Grove. We went over that Ash Grove, I'll remember it until . . . it was really something. He tried.[22]*

Of necessity, Mr. Wickett modeled for his 1940s music classes a circumstance that all would face at some time – making do with resources that in some cases were less than adequate. John

Robertson, who met his future wife Dorothy when they were students at the Normal School during its final year at Memorial Hall, recalled, "We used all the music books that were in the elementary schools, published in the year dot!"[23] Dorothy added, "But by the time we had them, they were on their last legs."[24]

Preparation was broadly based, aimed at both versatility and mastery. There was a certain logic to these performances that would relate directly to the actual practice of teaching:

> *Another thing about the Normal School experience that I do very clearly remember is that not only was it methodological, but we had lessons in public speaking. We were taught how to project our voice, and how to stand up properly. And we also had experience in conducting a choir. We had to stand up in front of the whole school and conduct the morning songs, and the Lord's Prayer, and so on. So that, it was just very, very classroom teacher practically oriented.[25]*

In large part, the weekly assemblies were intended to prepare the Normal School students preparation for the 'real life' of schools. As part of that requirement they offered practice in preparing for seasonal events that provided not only opportunities to mark and to celebrate, but also practice in managing events, a regular requirement for almost all teachers. On occasion, the regular flow of special events was interrupted by occurrences that also caught the attention of a far broader audience:

> *The Normal School itself put on this big Spring Concert, and, of course, and also a Christmas Concert, which was, you know, a big event for the school. That was the year that King George passed away, and the new Queen, and that was sort of a major event, especially for Victoria. And that year they didn't celebrate May Day because the city was in mourning . . . I know we had a day off, I was halfway up the hill when [my landlady] Marjorie shouted, "You'd better come back, everything's closed down today."[26]*

The Normal School curriculum included a course on the structure and operation of schools, an important learning component for these students. In many cases they would be forced to rely primarily on their own skills and wisdom in order to survive and succeed in their classrooms. Sadly, in this and other courses, content was sometimes overshadowed by style. Pat Floyd, an interviewee from the school's closing year, the 1955-56 class, was dubious about the vibrancy of what in his case was endured as a requirement rather than enjoyed as a valuable learning experience. Speaking of one of his instructors, he remembered that:

> He used to pontificate a lot. He taught us a course, I guess it was on ethics or something, school management, and management issues and ethical issues and so on. He used to stand in the front and just rattle off all these standards that he had and we were expected to follow them.[27]

That tone was set very early in the Normal School's history by instructors who ranged in skill and acceptance from the respected and fondly remembered to those whose students may have preferred to forget their contact.

In the early decades of the 1900s, British Columbia was a young, largely rural province with a great need for qualified teachers in its elementary schools. At the time the 1926-27 class attended, British Columbia's public school system had just undergone the sweeping and somewhat unfriendly scrutiny of the Putman Weir team. Percy Wilkinson (VPNS 1926-27) recalled a curriculum that was inclusive in content, perhaps in part as a response to the review. It also allowed some direct creative participation by the students:

> For instance, mathematics, or arithmetic, [and] grammar . . . was very important in those days, very important . . . we were all expected to be able to give some sort of instruction in painting . . . Miss Riddell was very successful, she taught the primary, mostly for the girls. We had a minimum . . . on primary instruction, but Miss Riddell taught us music, and she was very good at it . . . some of us, Harry Hickman and I and two others, formed a quartet, and performed for the student body from time to time. In fact, we quite enjoyed the music.[28]

The Model School

From the time of its construction until its temporary move during the Second World War, the Victoria Provincial Normal School had its own two-teacher instructional laboratory. A Department of Education document noted, "An elementary practice school or model school of two divisions is also housed in the Normal School building."[29] Marjorie (Thatcher) King, whose

1940-41 class was among the last to experience the Model School, remembered one of the teachers:

She did demonstration lessons. The children who came to the Model School were her pupils, and she did demonstration lessons. We may, I suppose we would have had lectures. But Primary Methods was one of the subjects that we were taught. And she would probably give us some lectures, and then she brought the children into the classroom and we would observe her teaching them.[30]

Division 2 of the Model School with teacher Miss James, 1942. Photo courtesy of UVic Archives, reference # 007.0707. Gibson's Studio photographer.

Model School pupils displaying projects, ca. 1940. Photo courtesy of UVic Archives, reference # 007.0709. Gibson's Studio photographer.

Some interviewees recalled that in the minds of parents, the Model School was a prestige placement for their children. Joe Lott recalled a theme perhaps echoed in today's overnight waits to be first in line for French immersion programs and magnet schools:

They had a Model School there which was very impressive. They had two teachers that I just thought were amazing in two classes. And we would observe occasionally these classes in progress. And apparently as far as parents were concerned, it was a real line-up to get your kids into that Model School.[31]

Unfortunately, when the Normal School relocated to Memorial Hall there was no space available for the Model School. It did not resume operation with the move back to the Lansdowne campus. A local paper noted in 1946 that as a result of the move, "no model school can be provided for normal school students . . . will necessitate the transportation of student teachers to city schools."[32] However, the former provision for demonstration lessons subsequently occurred in a new format. Bill Cross, who later became a teacher educator at the University of Victoria, remembered that:

Every week there were lessons put on in the auditorium, generally taught by one of the faculty, or taught by . . . a prominent teacher from the district, where they brought in a class and set it up and taught, and then you discussed it afterwards. Discussion was mainly faculty-led, and student-response.[33]

Opportunities for observation were not limited to classes brought in to the Normal School. Anne (Daser) Walters and her colleagues also observed in Victoria elementary schools:

They brought in classes to the Normal School a couple of times for us to observe, just for an hour or two in an afternoon, and then we went out and we observed in a few different schools, actually. And we got to observe the class that we were going to do our practicum with. That was just one week, the first one.[34]

Whatever their view of the Putman Weir report, faculty and administrators at the Victoria Provincial Normal School established as an operating principle that students would have opportunities to observe skilled senior colleagues in action. Though the opportunities and the format changed, that regularity was preserved throughout the life of the institution.

Physical Training and the Strathcona Trust

The Strathcona Trust has been well documented elsewhere. Its commitment was to enhance physical conditioning among young people. It became a strong and widespread movement supported by extensive programs, detailed curriculum materials, and certificates of achievement. Few of the interviewees remaining from the Normal School years recalled the Trust, though many could remember their experiences with physical education. Those from the class of 1926-27 also remembered that there had been a small pool, long since removed, in the gymnasium on the lower floor of the building.

From the early days, physical education classes at the two Normal Schools had a distinct military flavour. The operative term was "drill," and it implied a regimented, exercise-focused set of activities. The Normal Schools were present before and after two world wars, and in some years the drill included practice with mock rifles. Because Victoria was a military centre, there was a ready supply of armed forces instructors available and willing to instil a measure of fitness. References in principals' annual reports noted individuals of military rank who were assigned this duty; Ken Bradley recalled that in 1926-27, "We had a Sergeant from Military District Number 11 that came and instructed us... Oh, yes, he wouldn't stand any nonsense – Sergeant Bayne."[35] Joe

Girls gym class B, 1939-40. Photo courtesy of UVic Archives, reference # 007.0203.

Military drill with mock rifles, 1940-41. Photo courtesy of Marjorie King.

Lott recalled that by 1941-42, the experience was somewhat more positive, because "We had a drill sergeant from the Army, a very nice guy, who came up, 1 think, three times a week, who took the men, and put us through rather military-type physical education, jerks."[36]

The MacLean Method of Handwriting

Students attending Victoria Provincial Normal School in the fall of 1915 would have known Henry B. MacLean simply as one of their instructors. Shortly thereafter, he moved to the Vancouver Provincial Normal School, where he remained an instructor for many years. After 1921, decades of British Columbia elementary school students, though unfamiliar with the man, were well acquainted with his MacLean Method of Writing and its rigours. H.B. MacLean, the author of this system, saw it adopted by British Columbia elementary schools in 1921 as the approved style of penmanship both for elementary pupils and for teachers in training in British Columbia.

The MacLean Method of Handwriting remained the performance standard for British Columbia elementary school pupils for some thirty years. The method was supported by a series of compendiums that offered both clear models for emulation and opportunities for repeated practice. It was intended to produce a clear, flowing script; it endorsed sameness over originality in the interests of ensuring a common acceptable standard. Norma

(Matthews) Mickelson was among hundreds of Victoria Provincial Normal School students who were trained in the proper method:

> *And we got MacLean Method. Yes, exactly, and we were all taught how to teach writing, you know . . . you had to be able to balance an eraser on [the back of] your hand, and the pen had to held very loosely, and you did your ovals and your push and pulls and your letters.[37]*

Many students arrived at Normal School with memories of their own elementary school instruction in the MacLean Method, although some, including Pat Floyd, had adopted a more individualistic style since earning their certificates:

Maclean Method of Handwriting Compendiums.

> *One of my great regrets is that I've lost my MacLean Professional. I got the highest, the biggest certificate . . . They were really big, I always wanted to frame that and put it beside my degrees, because I thought it had a W. S. Gilbert sort of ring to it . . . Gilbert and Sullivan, you know . . . "writing in a hand so fine."*

> *One of the things that I got out of Normal School was how to write properly. I came into Normal School with the typical chicken scratch that most of us came out of high school with, and for some reason, I really caught on to doing my circles and "c's" and "b' s" and so on across the page, because we*

*actually did it in class . . . and it really benefitted me, because,
in those days, there were no computers. In fact, there were
hardly typewriters, so you did a lot of writing. And certainly
you wrote students' comments on report cards . . . and . . . in a
clear manner, which the MacLean Method certainly was.[38]*

In some cases, the benefits of that prior learning seemed to
have been lost over the intervening high school years, at least in
the view of some Normal School instructors. Normal School
certainly marked a return to MacLean's standards and
expectations, a return modelled on the approach that an
elementary classroom teacher might take with her own beginning
students. Anne (Daser) Walters discovered to her chagrin upon
arriving at Normal School that she and others were deemed to
have lost a certain degree of their previous skill, even though they
had received certificates:

*I know I had received one in grade school. I was so proud of
myself because I had gotten my Senior Certificate when I was
only in grade 6. So then it turned out to be quite a jolt when
they gave us the printing compendium to do first, at Normal
School, and I was criticized. . . . I thought I had done a good
job, but it wasn't good enough, anyway.[39]*

It seems to have been a part of the culture of teacher
education that some aspects of becoming a teacher required a
return to practices left behind at the end of childhood, practices
deemed by teacher educators to be essential to learning the craft.
Fortunately or unfortunately, there was for most, ample
opportunity to watch and try, again and again.

Observing and Practising

The observation and practice sequence began in the fall of the
Normal School year with classroom visits by the students. That
was followed by practica, first in the local area then farther afield,
often in a rural school. The pattern began early in the School's
history and, with some modification in the duration of its various
components, retained its essential structure – a phased
introduction to classroom practice. In 1926-27:

*Two by two students would go out to . . . classes to observe
certain lessons . . . we sat to one side. We took no part, of
course, and the teacher didn't introduce us or make any*

*reference . . . I don't recall if we had any particular
conversation with the teacher about what was being taught or
anything. But I do remember on one of those occasions . . . we
had questions to answer and we had to submit a report to the
Normal School staff about what we had seen and heard.*[40]

For some students, the experience of classroom visits was more
interactive. During one of Bill Cross' practica, the presence of
student teachers enabled the regular members of staff to
experiment with a then-innovative, now routine approach to
home-school liaison:

*they held an innovative thing at Lampson Street School. They
had parent-teacher interviews, the first in Victoria. And so they
took some of us as student-teachers to go and take the
teacher's class while the parent-teacher interviews went on.*[41]

Several interviewees recalled the value of their observation
and practice teaching. When they entered Normal School, most of
these student teachers had little prior background of involvement
with the classroom beyond their own years of schooling. The
intent of the teacher-training program, clearly, was that the
Normal School students would experience the range of likely
scenarios that they might encounter in their own classrooms:

*Our practice teaching, I think, was the key. When you had to
go to primary . . . you had a real look at children starting
school. I think all teachers should have to go to primary, teach
primary for a little while. And then, the next time we went to
intermediate, so that gave us an idea. And then the last time
we had to go out into the rural setting. It wasn't a surprise.*[42]

In the mid-1940s, "rural" held a different connotation than we
grant it today. Certainly British Columbia was more rural than not,
a situation that still characterizes, geographically at least, a large
portion of the province. Not all rural areas, though, were remote.
Metchosin, Sooke, and the Saanich Peninsula, areas now within
30 minutes of downtown Victoria, offered a rural teaching
experience to complement the earlier observation and practicum
sessions carried out in the schools of Victoria. Dorothy (Millner)
Robertson from the class of 1945-46 described the sequence that
began with silent observation followed by the initial practice
experience:

*And one in March. And then just after Easter, you had your
choice. The idea was to go to a rural school, and many of the*

*people who were from the Interior went back to their
hometowns to do their practice teaching, or else they went to
a rural school like Metchosin, or Sooke, or whatever, here.[43]*

The process of observation that preceded and accompanied
practice teaching was a two-phase affair. When the practicum
began, the observer became the observed:

*The teacher whose class you were taking would watch you,
especially the first few days to see if there were any problems,
and, I guess, discipline was the main concern – could you
handle the class? They would then tend to go off and do their
own thing. They would drop in and out of your class, and they
would do a report on your performance. And then a member of
the faculty or one of the teachers of the Normal School would
come along and observe you for a good chunk of time, two or
three hours, usually, I think.[44]*

In the early years at least, the post-practicum sequence was
quite definite. After the practicum, the results were delivered by
Normal School officials in formal fashion:

*You would get a notice. You'd line up, your name was on the
board...a certain time to go to whoever. Well, they would get
the reports back from the teacher if they were not able to get
there themselves . . . you'd go in . . . and discuss the matter, as
to where you failed, and where you forgot something, or
where you excelled, if you did.[45]*

The practicum experience was a source of anxiety for many.
The students were very aware of being "on display," not only in
front of the class, but also before often exacting observers –
certainly the classroom teacher, and usually a Normal School
instructor also. Memories of these experiences, particularly the
areas in which they may have fallen short of their own or others'
expectations, remained fresh many years later for many, including
Anne (Daser) Walters:

*To start, I missed the bus. It had rerouted and I didn't know. To
make it worse . . . my homeroom teacher drove by and
frowned at me! I was so nervous, it was just pathetic. I
actually pretended I was sick the last two days. I just couldn't
see it through, you know. And, yes, the person who did come
to see me gave me, I would say, no encouragement . . . And I
remember her saying, "Now you just have to speak totally*

correctly. Do you know that three times, maybe twice, in the time I was there, you said, 'jist' instead of 'just?' Now you must not do that."[46]

The challenge of precision seemed to have been universal and often unattainable. The focus was frequently on diction. Pat Floyd, a student from the Normal School's final year, found some humour in his particular violation, because "I remember I used to say 'pro-noun-ciation' instead of 'pronunciation,' and I got called to task for mispronouncing pronunciation."[47]

Not only pronunciation was considered important – protocol and propriety were also essential. Sadly, on the worst of occasions our best efforts can sometimes fall prey to our shortcomings in regard to approved procedure. On one such occasion, young Joe Lott's effort at creative accommodation was seen by his supervising teacher to have violated the norms of professional practice. Joe's attempt to compensate for an equipment shortage was not received with enthusiasm by his critical audience:

My first [practicum] was at Lampson Elementary School in Esquimalt. And I committed a cardinal sin there that I was reprimanded for. I was asked to teach about the lever. And I didn't have any equipment with me, so I took a long ruler off a blackboard railing . . . I took some books off the shelf, and I demonstrated to the little children how a lever worked . . . And afterward the teacher motioned me, "You don't do that with books. You don't put them on the floor – they're the most wonderful things for the children."[48]

Not everyone was nervous, but most encountered the usual range of challenges that arise from lack of experience. The Normal School students were well instructed in the allocation of time, at least in terms of the weekly minutes of instruction required in their classroom timetables. The expectations were clear:

We did lesson plans for our practicum . . . the whole issue of lesson plans was very, very important, and timetabling. And before we left Normal School, we had to make a timetable up, and it had to have . . . the Department of Education's prescribed number of minutes for each subject. And . . . when I was there, we had to make up timetables for a one-grade situation, for a two-grade situation, and, I can still remember, for a four-grade situation . . . and we had to have those . . .

exact, to the minute. So, we all started out with either
Arithmetic or Reading, five days a week . . . followed by
something else, and then there'd be recess, and those minutes
had to balance. We had to have that many minutes. And we
had to do that for one grade, two grades, and four grades. I
don't know what happened to the poor teachers that went out
to teach eight grades.[49]

Carefully crafted timetables, though, could not always be
translated into brilliantly timed lessons, particularly in the short
and somewhat artificial practicum experience. As Joe Lott
discovered, timing was crucial:

I was fortunate because I didn't have the qualms that many
had, getting up in front of a class. I didn't perform any better,
but the initial getting up on my feet didn't worry me too much.
I can remember one or two times I ran far over time and had
far too much material. Of course, I was criticized for not
keeping an eye on time.[50]

Sometimes the problem was not with personal time
management skills at lesson time, but with planning work for a
group of pupils whose skills were relatively unfamiliar to the
novice practitioner. On those occasions, it was important to have
an abundance of what was referred to as 'seatwork.' That meant
extending an already heavy load of lesson preparation to ensure
enrichment, busy-ness, or at least order in the classroom while the
teacher was occupied with groups or individuals.

In the middle years of the Normal School period, early
technology became available for seatwork production. For busy
teachers, the 'jelly pad' was a welcome advance. The jelly pad
was a predecessor to the more technically advanced spirit
duplicator and eventually the photocopier and the computer's
companion printer. It contained a stiff jellied compound in a tray
that resembled a cookie sheet. To produce a copy, the teacher
placed an original upside down on the jelly pad and smoothed the
reverse side of the paper, transferring an image to the surface of
the jelly pad. The image could then be transferred repeatedly to
plain sheets of paper as handouts for pupil use. For Norma
(Matthews) Mickelson and her colleagues, using this technology
to produce copies for her practicum class was an effective
strategy. Her students, though, were more than ready for the

challenge of dealing with her carefully prepared material:

My lasting memory with Parksville [Elementary School] is the old jelly pad . . . trying to get materials for the students to work on, because you had four grades . . . teaching reading was big. And you would work until midnight getting stuff done on the old jelly pad . . . And you'd get it out to the grade ones . . . And they'd finish it in two minutes.[51]

The spirit duplicator marked the next generation of in-school printing equipment. It appeared first as a hand-cranked device and later as an electrically powered machine that could produce multiple copies from an original. In lineage, both machines were ancestors of today's photocopier. Both reproduced the teacher's writing, typing, or sketches as a purple image on a stencil that could be reproduced. The difficulty of using the stencil, if one touched it on the active surface, was that it also produced purple stains on skin and clothing. Given the prevalence in schools of white shirts for men and white blouses for women, these machines were often viewed with annoyance by teachers, referred to by more than one as "the devil's own devices." However, the spirit duplicator, and even the jelly pad, were invaluable aids for busy classroom teachers, especially those facing the demands of multi-grade classrooms.

The students' practicum placements in rural classrooms not only introduced them to the realities of the multi-grade classroom, it made some aware of a shortcoming of the Normal School program. Despite the emphasis on calculating and allocating the correct number of minutes across the subjects, there was little practical preparation for dealing with the complex settings many would face. The reality of rural schools was duly noted, but some attempts to provide necessary management skills fell short of being truly helpful. The problem was particularly acute in the early years, when the rural setting was the norm:

Recognizing the fact that most of us were going to go into the country, they arranged for us to go and teach in Saanich . . . I had gone to Saanichton School briefly in 1915, . . . so I asked if I might go out there again, because a friend of mine was then principal of the two-room school. So that was easily arranged . . . I didn't teach all day, but I taught every other class, perhaps. I think there were . . . two of us teaching at the same time . . . it gave us five days contact with the routine in . . . a rural school, well, as close as they could get to Victoria. But for those who were going to a one-room school . . . it really wasn't much help . . . Nearly all . . . went to a school where you have got three or four grades in one room, and there was nothing at the Normal School that ever . . . indicated . . . how you would cope with it - what do you do?[52]

Interviewees' memories offered rich opportunities for insight into their early teaching experiences. They remembered much, especially of the human interactions that shaped their Normal School days. Ken Bradley recalled being summoned to Principal Vernon Denton's office after teaching a lesson, one that both considered to have been a less than stellar performance. He and others recalled, even many years later, the crusty administrator's human side:

It was English Literature, and I can't teach Literature. I can teach Social Studies or Science or Music, but I don't understand what these poets mean. So, shall I tell you what Denton told me? . . . He called me into his office when we got back . . . and he said, "You made a hell of a mess of that one, didn't you?" . . . I thought, you know, because this happened in the spring it's going to have an awful effect on my results.

So I kind of apologized to him, and said, "English Literature is not my thing." "Well," he said, "don't think because I teach Geography and History that I don't know anything about English Literature . . . because I do." Quite definite about it. And then all of a sudden he burst out laughing and said, "Okay, Okay," and waved me out. He was a character. But, you know, the memories that man left with you.[53]

Ken's final remark was similar to the comments of others about instructors who had revealed characteristics that they in turn sought to emulate in their own classrooms. Those memories were included with others less human, more managerial, and for some, equally memorable.

A Balanced Register

Teachers in most jurisdictions are required to maintain an accurate record of student attendance. Virtually every interviewee recalled the task of keeping the register. Whether the register was kept as a Normal School exercise or in one's own classroom, it was an important and symbolic ritual. Those who attended the Normal School learned the record-keeping exercise by maintaining a register for their class of in-training colleagues as though it was their own elementary school class. Norma (Matthews) Mickelson recalled, "And, of course, our class register, that was our class, those were the people – we kept that register."[54] Joe Lott agreed, remarking, "Oh, how true. How carefully we filled those damned things out, eh? Little crosses, et cetera."[55]

Norma remembered at least one instructor as being meticulous about how the Normal School students must keep their registers:

> *Yes, that's what he did. And as I say, it was really . . . picture perfect, it was pretty. Little tiny squares with these crosses, one line for morning, one line for afternoon, dot for late, and another dot for late, that's late in the afternoon, late in the morning. I mean, it was really pretty.*[56]

The practice continued when Norma moved into her teaching career. An accurate monthly record was essential, and the task could assume a monumental significance at year-end:

> *Registers had to be perfect, perfect. And, of course . . . you didn't leave at the end of June until you gave your register to the principal, and he checked it and it was okay. You didn't leave the school until that was right.*[57]

The overall quality of teachers' record-keeping and reporting was often criticized by British Columbia's school inspectors in the 1800s, when first efforts were being made to establish a public school system that would be not only accessible but also accountable. Grants were related to enrolments, and legal problems could arise if the record was not accurate. It became clear to all that the register was an essential element in gaining the grants and avoiding the problems.

Even many years later, Marjorie (Thatcher) King recalled that the register was a vital document, "Because you had all these columns to add up and you had to even up sideways and up and down, and if you made a bit of a mistake, you had to do it all over again."[58] Pat Floyd also realized the impact of an unbalanced register – his June pay cheque was held until his balanced register was accepted:

> *I remember the first year of teaching I was out half a day, and*

it took me half a day to find my half-day . . . It had to balance before you'd get your final cheque. And you had to do monthly reports, of course. We didn't get our final cheque until the year balanced, in June . . . The principal sat there with the cheque and you didn't get your cheque until you brought your balanced register, and it balanced with your monthly report. As I said, I was out half a day somewhere in one of the months. I made a half-day error, and it took me half a day to figure out where it was.[59]

They were trained well, both in the mechanics of classroom management and in the expectations for their performance both in and out of school. Like teachers everywhere, they understood that theirs was a noble venture – the students were their first priority. For Pat Floyd, the matter of commitment had already been settled when he embarked on his career:

Always do your duty. Even if the principal tells you to do something that you recognize is not ethically or morally correct, you must do the ethical or moral or legal responsibility. So, if you're out supervising classes and the principal wants you to come to a meeting, and it's your responsibility, really, to be looking after those children, you stay with the children. I remember that one.[60]

For many, commitment would be tested in the crucible of experiences they had not imagined when they entered Normal School. For a few, the venture was not destined to last. For many, it would be a rewarding career filled with recollections of children and a lifetime of stories. For almost all, it was marked by memories forged in moments in time. As Sylvia (Bradwell) Kelly recalled in a poem written at the time of the 50th reunion of the class of 1945-46, "We studied together for only one year, but our lives intertwined and friendships grew dear."[61]

Notes to Chapter 6

1 *BCGN 4:5*, May 1956, 8.
2 Putman Weir, 231).
3 Ibid., 231.
4 Ibid., 231.
5 Ibid., 207.
6 Pat Floyd 2002.
7 Ibid.
8 Marjorie (Thatcher) King 2003.
9 Norma (Matthews) Mickelson 2002.
10 Anne (Daser) Walters 2002.
11 Percy Wilkinson 2002.
12 Pat Floyd 2002.
13 Norma (Matthews) Mickelson 2002.
14 Marjorie (Thatcher) King 2003.
15 Bill Cross 2002.
16 Jim Whyte 2002.
17 Norma (Matthews) Mickelson 2002.
18 Ibid.
19 Joe Lott 2002.
20 Sylvia Kelly (nee Bradwell), *An Ode to the Class of '46*, unpublished poem distributed at class reunion, 1996.
21 Norma (Matthews) Mickelson 2002.
22 Marjorie (Thatcher) King 2003.
23 John Robertson 2002.
24 Dorothy (Millner) Robertson 2002.
25 Norma (Matthews) Mickelson 2002
26 Anne (Daser) Walters 2002.
27 Pat Floyd 2002.
28 Percy Wilkinson 2002.
29 Department of Education, *Regulations and Courses of Study for Provincial Normal Schools 1928-29* (Victoria: Department of Education, 1928).
30 Marjorie (Thatcher) King 2003.
31 Joe Lott 2002.
32 *Victoria Daily Times* (Victoria, BC), 16 October 1946.
33 Bill Cross 2002.
34 Anne (Daser) Walters 2002.
35 Ken Bradley 2002.
36 Joe Lott 2002.
37 Norma (Matthews) Mickelson 2002.
38 Pat Floyd 2002.
39 Anne (Daser) Walters 2002.
40 Percy Wilkinson 2002.
41 Bill Cross 2002.
42 John Robertson 2002.
43 Dorothy (Millner) Robertson 2002.
44 Pat Floyd 2002.
45 Percy Wilkinson 2002.
46 Anne (Daser) Walters 2002.
47 Pat Floyd 2002.
48 Joe Lott 2002.
49 Norma (Matthews) Mickelson 2002.
50 Joe Lott 2002.
51 Norma (Matthews) Mickelson 2002.
52 Percy Wilkinson 2002.
53 Ken Bradley 2002.
54 Norma (Matthews) Mickelson 2002.
55 Joe Lott 2002.
56 Norma (Matthews) Mickelson 2002.
57 Ibid.
58 Marjorie (Thatcher) King 2003.
59 Pat Floyd 2002.
60 Pat Floyd 2002.
61 Sylvia Kelly (nee Bradwell), *An Ode to the Class of '46*, unpublished poem distributed at class reunion, 1996.

LEARNING TO TEACH

TEACHER PREPARATION
IN VICTORIA, BC
1903-1963

Chapter 7
Out There:
Life in Classroom and Community

From the beginning, the Victoria Provincial Normal School drew almost all of its candidates from the rural regions of British Columbia. Once certified, many would return to the rural areas, whether by design or by necessity, to practice their craft. Some were able, if they wished, to return to their home areas, or at least to similar communities. Many, though, preferred to strike out on their own as young adults. Some found great success and rich careers; others were disappointed and dismayed at the stark realities they encountered. From the vantage point of distance and years, we might argue that it was attitude – a spirit of adventure – that made the crucial difference. The challenges facing these young teachers, though, were real and acute. Many of them were socially, culturally, even emotionally isolated from the familiarity of old friends and former surroundings. In this chapter I will recount some of their stories with the hope that reading these accounts will inform the reader who is unfamiliar with both the years and the experiences. Beyond that, I hope that readers who have "been there" will be reminded of their own stories, anecdotes perhaps forgotten with the passage of time.

Throughout the years of the Victoria Provincial Normal School's existence, and particularly in the early years, a picture is painted of creative, committed individuals who experienced much that was surprising, elements that were thoroughly enjoyable, and sometimes overwhelming loneliness and despair. In a 1922 letter, Lorraine Johns wrote of her first-year experience to her Normal School friend Lillian Anderson that:

The school itself is a weird frame building – very small – it is of course only one room – nothing like a hall, porch or school yard. There is a huge mountain at the back and timber – timber all around. Inside there is a narrow strip of cloth blackboard that simply won't look black. One window is broken so we have pretty good ventilation. There is only one outhouse and it has no door.

Of course, the school is awfully poorly equipped – 1 or 2 maps. I have to draw the others on the frightfully inadequate blackboard. I would be at sea completely if I had not brought my normal school books along . . .

It took me two days to get from Bella Coola to this god forsaken place – we came most of the way by prairie schooner

. . .There are numerous coyotes and grizzlys [sic] about here – there was a coyote drinking out of the spring behind the school one day . . . I have to keep my babies at school until 3:30 [probably to ensure they would be accompanied by older children] because they met a grizzly on the way home one night . . . they fled howling and hid for an hour until some of the older pupils found them . . .

This is an awfully lonesome place – there are only about 5 families and they are scattered over some 10 miles or so – there is nothing like a store – Fords, dancing, etc. are almost things unknown. I sometimes wonder if I won't go crazier than I am – I am frightfully homesick – weep foolishly and feel worse . . . I merely exist for the mail. Loads of love, Laurie.[1]

Laurie's stay in Firvale was short. The friend who forwarded her letter to the Archives notes, "She only wrote once – did not finish the term."[2] Laurie apparently left the area for California, where she met and married a dentist, presumably one practising in a more hospitable area and climate.

A few years later, a young woman in the Cariboo faced a more immediate and critical problem. Rural schools in many cases were small one-room log structures heated by a pot-bellied stove with a stovepipe through the roof. It was important both to keep the room warm and to do so safely, and that unfortunately was not always the case. Fire, of course, was a dread enemy in the days when there was virtually no way of dealing with it effectively. Perhaps the only reason more did not die as fire victims was that these were such uncomplicated buildings, as Lorraine Johns had noted (though hers was not a log building) – one room, no halls, and a single door. Marjorie (Campbell) Brown (VPNS 1926-27), in retrospect at least, seems to have handled her emergency situation quite calmly:

> The school burned down over my head when I had been there about a month, I guess. It turned cold, and one of the men around came and put the fire on, and I happened to look up, and here it was all burning all around the stovepipe. So I just told the kids to go and get their coats, and to go outside. And that was it...One-room school...Log...And then after that, we moved into one half of a house. There was an old chap living in the other half. And that's where we had our school for the year. And then a year or two later my dad was up there and he built them a proper school.[3]

One thing these early one-room schools did not include was an indoor toilet facility. In fact, virtually no one could have conceived of such a luxury. Even the passage of time and modern advances elsewhere did not take care of that situation in all cases. Almost 30 years later, outhouses were still a reality in some locales, despite promises and best efforts. Some whose stories I have recorded recalled their experiences with these primitive facilities that have become the subject of much humour and more than one book.

Finding a Job

For years, beginners in many fields have been told that employers need people with experience. They have also received little help or encouragement in response to their question, "But how do I get it?" The experience of teachers with issues of supply and demand has varied over the years, shaped by a variety of uncontrollable and often frustrating factors: population growth and shrinkage, public policy changes, and social trends, to name a few. Many new teachers have realized that they must go for their first years of experience to the places where jobs were available. For many, the 1927 experience of one young Normal School graduate has a still-familiar ring:

> And so many applications I wrote, I was told . . . we need experienced teachers. That was the big thing . . . But we've got

*to get our experience somewhere. So I went away off into the
bush, northwest of Prince George . . . Reid Lake . . . One room
school . . . In my way of thinking, that was the only weak side
of the Normal School instruction. We were, I would say, very
well prepared for a graded school, but we weren't that well
prepared for landing in a school where you have grades 1 to
8.[4]*

Not all found their first jobs, even in rural communities, far
removed from their family homes. Many of their stories, and some
of their job offers, arose out of the issues of the day. In the early
years, though primary teaching was thought handled best by
women, that preference clearly was limited to single women. It
would be many years, certainly after one interviewee's 1941 story,
before married women were welcome in the classroom. In some
cases, if a woman hoped to continue teaching, her marital status
would have to remain a secret. Perhaps in more instances than
were revealed, the plan succeeded. If it did not, the woman would
be required to leave her position. That was the consequence for
one woman whose blessed event turned misfortune worked to the
advantage of her young student teacher Marjorie (Thatcher) King:

*And then at the end of the year, I went to Cassidy to do my
final practicum. And it was rather interesting. It was quite
near where my home was, and I knew the people there, and
they knew that I was going to be a teacher. And the teacher
who had been there for a number of years had got married
secretly at Christmastime . . . in those days, married teachers
couldn't teach at all . . . And come spring time she found she
was pregnant, and she had to leave. So, she asked me if I
would come, and I took over the class when I got through at
Normal School, for May and June.[5]*

With the coming of World War II, things began to change. One
of the variable realities of teaching, supply and demand, altered
the picture drastically for many seeking teaching positions. In
some ways, it was the beginning of a new era for women such as
Dorothy (Millner) Robertson in the search for a career in the
schools:

*There certainly weren't any married women in Victoria, except
widows. I would suspect that the reason the change came
about, and the reason that the teaching profession made such
advances as far as women were concerned, was because of the*

baby boom and such a shortage of teachers. And they had to have them - it was a necessity.[6]

For both men and women, the end of the war signalled a new era in business, industry, and the schools. Just before that, though, it was not particularly a buyer's market for employers. The schools were not exempt from the problem:

They were drawing on the people that were available during the war, or right at the end of the war. So, there was reason, I suppose, to wonder at the qualifications. But they were . . . taking what was available.[7]

Not all unexpected job offers arose as a result of social norms or working conditions of the day. In some cases, chance meetings and casual conversations led to offers of work. Joe Lott decided to explore possibilities away from the classroom. He took a job in the financial industry for a time, then through an unplanned but ultimately fortunate conversation, changed direction:

I continued university, got a bachelor of commerce degree, and was going to take the business world by storm, because personnel offices were beginning to bloom in the industrial and commercial world and I wanted to be a personnel officer. . . . I went to work for the Royal Trust at $100.00 a month. And I was walking along Government Street one lunch hour and bumped into this drill sergeant from the [Normal School], which had been five years before or something.

We chatted, and he said, "How are you doing, how do you like it," et cetera. And I said I wasn't very happy, but it was a nice place to work . . . it was real unchallenging work. And anyway, he said to me, ""Would you be interested in a teaching job?" And I said, "What is it?" And he said, "It's teaching senior boys Phys Ed in Port Alberni."

And then he dropped the bomb - $1800 a year! I was getting $1200! $600 doesn't sound like much . . . But it was an enormous difference in those days. And Rita and I were planning to get married . . . and we decided, let's go to Alberni and we'll take the $1800 a year So, it's one of those little accidents of life that change your whole life pattern.[8]

Joe's first teaching job offer had also contained a salary surprise. This was an era of variability across the province, and some chances were simply too good to turn down:

He said, "I have an opening to teach my grade 4-5-6 class, and some high school Phys Ed. Would you be interested?" I said, "Yes, I would." He said, "The salary will be $900 a year." Well, the going rates were $600-$700, maybe, if you were lucky, $800. Nine hundred, my God!

Hedley was a booming mining town, and the Mascot Nickel Plate mines were bustling, the war was on . . . There was a railway line came up the Similkameen Valley, right to Hedley . . . Hedley was prosperous. So, off I went end of September . . . midnight boat from Victoria, off at the other end at 7 in the morning. Up the ramp to the railway station, ticket on the Kettle Valley Express, and waited around until it left, and then through the mountains arriving in Princeton, I think. It was just after four in the morning, and then off there with your bags. Wait for the bus . . . down the north side of the Similkameen River on a gravel road.

I arrive at Hedley. There, Howard Denton [school principal] is waiting for me. Takes me over to the hotel, and into the beer parlour, I had never been to a beer parlour in my life, golden-haired little boy from Victoria. Orders us a beer. But anyway, then I registered in the hotel for a couple of nights to find accommodation.

Howard helping me, we found a little cabin. Had two rooms, front room with a bed and an old chesterfield, and a back room with a kitchen sink and cupboards and a coal and wood stove. And the outhouse was 50 feet away . . . You understand that the temperatures in Hedley in the wintertime dropped to minus 35 Fahrenheit. And going to the outhouse was a strenuous experience. But you cooked for yourself, you used the sponge bath over the kitchen sink to clean yourself up and shave. And off you went in your suit and shirt and tie and went to work. I taught grade 4, 5, and 6, and three or four times I got the whole high school, which went from 7 to 12 . . . across the road to the Community Hall, and I would teach this whole cluster of older kids Phys Ed. . . . quite a year for a young guy. I was 19 years old, and it was just great, a bustling little mining town. And I've marveled over the years since, at those two high school teachers, all the subjects from grades 7 to 12, about 30 to 35 kids. And just mind-boggling when you think about it . . .

I had marvelous adventures, horse-riding which I had never done before, and hiking in the Interior . . . it was a great year for me. But, towards the end of it, I said to myself, "Gosh, you've got to get more education." I didn't have a target then or anything, but I realized I needed more education if I was going to do anything interesting in education. So I went back to Victoria . . . I was offered the job of principal if I wanted to stay [in Hedley], can you imagine? But that's a sign of the day, men were scarce as could be, and there wouldn't be any thought of making a woman principal in those days.[9]

Getting There

In the early days, transportation options were limited and roads in some cases were nonexistent. Arrangements were made by letter or by telegram, and changing one's plans could result in unanticipated problems. Ken Bradley, who began his teaching career in 1927, recalled his inauspicious arrival at a community in remote northern British Columbia.[10] His first choice, and his announced plan, had been "to go by train Vancouver to Red Pass Junction, and then back on the Prince Rupert train, get off west of Prince George, and walk north." He had a change of heart and decided, "I would rather go by boat to Prince Rupert, and take the train the other way." Anxious not to cause difficulties for the welcoming party, "I telegraphed them that... instead of 9 o'clock at night, I would be arriving the following morning at 6 o'clock." However, his plans fell victim to a transportation problem, and "As luck would have it, the boat was cancelled. It was a CN steamer, and I had to go by train. So it didn't click... They didn't meet me." Undaunted, he walked the eight miles from the train station to "an opening with a few log houses, a school."

Percy Wilkinson recounted the adventures of some of his colleagues, young teachers who realized not only the challenges they faced beginning their careers far from home, but also the sparse existence of the locals:

There were various difficulties. Some people had to go up to Edmonton and take the railway into the Peace River, and go from there. In many cases, they were absolutely isolated, and once you got there you were there, on a whistle stop on the railway line for the year. One or two teachers were concerned about the absolute lack of any reading material, and went out of their own pockets to acquire books and so on to be sent out up there, so that people would have things to read. Yes, they had amazing stories.[11]

The people living in these remote areas were homesteaders trying, not always with great success, to eke out a living from the land. Work was their life, and all too often there was little time for socializing with the lonely souls who came to teach their children:

Mainly, they tried to farm after they cut the bush down. And, in the wintertime when they couldn't farm (and winter began at the end of September), they would cut ties for the railway . . . A woman [was there before me]. I was the second teacher . . . She'd lasted six months . . . I think it was the isolation.[12]

For some, the rural adventure held great appeal. John Jackson moved from the city for a short exchange period and a stimulating change of surroundings:

I ended up out in the bush, after university, outside of Quesnel at Bouchie Lake. . . . This was a high point of challenge and enjoyment and change . . . I took the train to Quesnel, and then . . . a taxi to a boarding house outside, not far from Bouchie Lake. And I walked the distance to the school, which was a one-room school, pot-bellied stove at the back, eight grades, 15 students, and all in one room. I enjoyed it.[13]

Things changed in rural British Columbia, but not rapidly. Teachers two decades later still had to cope with the challenges of rural life. In some cases, more hospitable circumstances prevailed. The stories, though, continued as these young people faced the challenges of working in communities often far from home and frequently as diverse in their populations as in their geographic locations.

Classroom Challenges

Teaching in rural British Columbia in the first half of the 20th century typically meant having a wide range of ages and grades, and closely related families. The school facilities were limited – perhaps a one-or two-room school and an outhouse. There was certainly wildlife, and support from the community could be mixed. Anne (Daser) Walters began her career in 1942 in the tiny Cariboo community of Miocene, a short distance from Horsefly and a longer trek from Williams Lake. She recalled a pleasant start:

> *A one-room log school, yes - eight grades. It was a good community to be in. All the children except two were cousins of a big extended family, and they were basically, you know, kind, understanding people. It was good, that way, yes. I boarded about two miles away from the school, with a widow and her daughter. And I walked back and forth. It was a really good place to be . . . I felt very at home there, and enjoyed it.[14]*

A few years later, just after the end of World War Two, Kay (Kennedy) Hinkes began her career of many years' teaching in the South Cariboo region of the province:

> *My first year of teaching was an adventure full of new territory, laughter, tricks, and good friends.*
>
> *The school was a one-room log structure, heated by a barrel stove. There was no inside plumbing, but a his and hers outside facility was available. Water came by buckets from the Bonaparte River.*
>
> *In the winter when it was anywhere from -20 to -60 F, our lunches, which were on a shelf at the back of the room, froze. Opening the door of the barrel stove, we toasted our sandwiches. To this day I cannot eat sardines. There is nothing worse than toasted sardine sandwiches![15]*

John Robertson began a similar adventure in the southern interior of the province in 1946. He recalled the pragmatic necessities of organizing the classroom in ways that would enable him to accomplish his work:

> *Between Castlegar and Nelson, just north of South Slocan, or east of South Slocan. A one-room school, eight grades. Some of the kids in grade 8 were the same age as me. One boy in grade 4 who I promoted to grade 5 . . . to cut down on my teaching preparation load.[16]*

The challenges of the multi-grade classroom demanded of these beginning teachers a level of experience and skill that they simply would have to acquire on the spot. Planning was the key, and some rural classrooms were models for the development of cooperative learning initiatives. Put simply, success demanded the willing participation and support of everyone in the classroom.

Teachers such as John Robertson became masters of the art:

When you get into a rural school, of grades 1 to 8, you certainly develop the technique of getting everybody to work together. I can still remember one of the first things I learned was, whenever anybody's finished their work, you'd better go over and have one of the grade 1's read to you, or the grade 2's read to you, or the grade 3's read to you. I don't think the grade 1's ever stopped reading – I don't know if they did anything else all day but read to somebody – there was always somebody finished.[17]

Often it was the teacher who was most conscious of age – his or her own. Most of these beginners were young, some just a year out of high school themselves. I can recall sitting on the steps of my boarding house at the age of almost 18, hearing one of my students call to his friend as they passed by, "That's where the old man lives." Thinking of the incident much later, I understood the reflections of Pat Floyd, who completed Normal School a few years before me:

I was 18. I turned 19 later that year, and I was in the secondary part of the school, so I taught Music to the grade 7 and 8 students as well as my grade 6 class, and I coached the senior boys' basketball team . . . I had a kid on the team that was older than I was . . . and I had children from age 9 to 16, in the one class . . . I had four or five young girls who had been promoted a year, so they were a year ahead of their peers . . . mostly immigrant kids . . . in those days, if you were functioning at a grade 6 level, you went to grade 6, and one of them was 16 years old. Here I was 18 years old, and I had a girl 16 years old in my class.[18]

Not every school was as rural. Port Alberni, during the war years, for example, may not have had all the facilities of a city, but it was marked by an air of activity and prosperity despite somewhat makeshift school facilities:

A really bustling mill town. They were building the pulp mill then . . . all the classrooms were army huts, and the gymnasium where I spent most of my time, was a large old army workshop, a huge place. They'd put basketball hoops up, et cetera, and I took the senior boys (you didn't have mixed classes there), senior boys Phys Ed, in the old army hall up above the camp. Anyway, that, too, was an interesting year.[19]

These teachers, in most cases, were self-reliant people with the confidence and energy of youth. They believe they had been taught their craft well, and this was the opportunity to prove their worth:

I felt competent in my first year of teaching with three grades in one classroom and 29 kids. I didn't have any major problems. I'd been well instructed in lesson preparation and so on, and I felt I was a qualified teacher.[20]

Beyond lesson preparation and multi-grade classes, toilet facilities were often a part of the interviewees' stories. Whole books have been written about outhouses, a feature stamped indelibly in the minds and olfactory memories of many rural children, their families, and their teachers. John Jackson was determined to make the best of a less than desirable situation. In a true spirit of cooperative learning, he involved the students in sweetening their own environment:

The outdoor facility was in a dreadful mess. I got some Lysol and cleared out everything, laid the law down, and said, "This is the way it's going to be." So... the chaps [maintenance workers] came in with the water supply once a week, a milk can for drinking and a milk can for washing. And I was my own janitor. So these men had a smile on their face in the back of the room, "We'd like you to know you have the sweetest smelling outhouse in the Quesnel district."[21]

Virtually every school now, even in the most remote and isolated parts of the province, has adequate plumbing facilities. Change, though, was often slow in coming and was often accompanied by unanticipated problems:

I started teaching at a two-room school in South Wellington when it was still rural. And, indeed, they promised me in the job interview that they would install flush toilets when I got there. But when I got there, they had made the mistake of drilling a little more deeply to get a greater flow of water, and they broke into an old mine shaft underneath and lost the water. And so that school survived on outhouses as long as I was there. It led to all kinds of interesting experiences.[22]

Using the term loosely, some might still call parts of the Saanich Peninsula just outside Victoria, rural. Today it is an area of suburban mixed economy, a comfortable near-town locale that still maintains a flavour and an aroma of agriculture and country fairs. Its communities, though, offer a far different experience today from that of the Normal School graduates who went there to teach, including Joe Lott:

Saanichton was a two-room school, and I had grades 4, 5, and 6 again. And they had two outhouses, so it was back to Hedley days. There was a girls' outhouse, and a boys' outhouse. And I had three or four delightful years there, and then I moved to North Saanich.[23]

It seems reasonable to assume that "three or four delightful years" referred to the school, not to the "facilities!" The facilities, though, were accepted as the norm, as was the provision for drinking water, which did not always follow our present understanding of safety and hygiene:

Bucket of water with a dipper in it, I think. There was a girl who was a kind of a janitor, she used to come in the morning. There was a pot-bellied stove with a little pile of wood beside it, and a stand with a bucket of water with a dipper. And that's what the children, everybody, used – the same dipper, I'm afraid, to have a drink of water.[24]

As dippers preceded drinking fountains and outhouses preceded flush toilets, so walking, catching the bus, and hitching a ride preceded having one's own car to drive. Marjorie (Thatcher) King recalled:

My parents are pioneers in the area up there, and so it was kind of neat that I was teaching there to start with. I had to walk. From home to Cassidy was about . . . four or five miles . . . . Well, I didn't walk every day. because I got lucky...From home up to the highway, it was about a half mile, and I walked that every day, but then when I got on the highway, the McGavin's bread man used to pick me up sometimes, and if he didn't get me, the telephone truck guys always used to pick me up and give me a ride . . . They got used to me going along the highway . . . when I was teaching at Ladysmith. I had to take the bus . . . from South Wellington to Ladysmith, it was nine miles. I took the Island Coach Lines.[25]

Not all of these teachers found work in rural communities. Some began their teaching in more urban settings such as

Victoria. The city offered a different social setting than that of interior British Columbia, and it had its own rules and expectations for a young beginning teacher's decorum. Norma (Matthews) Mickelson recalled:

I was the only young person on that staff. There were two men, and all the rest were women. And I can still remember, as a very young person (I was only 18), going into the staff room . . . there was a little can of Pacific Milk in the fridge, and taking that out and putting it on the table for recess . . . One of the teachers came in, took one look at that, picked it up, put it back in the fridge, and told me that we never, never put a can of milk on the table . . . And, to this day, I can't do it . . . I have to use a cream pitcher. But that comes back to the deportment thing, you know, how you were supposed to act as a teacher.[26]

Urbanness did not necessarily guarantee better school facilities. In fact, some classrooms facilities were downright unpleasant, as Marjorie (Thatcher) King experienced in the early 1940s:

I had a very difficult time in the last year that I taught in Coquitlam because I was given a classroom which was down in the basement. It was L-shaped, and the blackboard was across the one part, and the classroom was L-shaped . . . and it had posts in the middle. And there were tables and chairs for the students, rather than desks . . . enough tables and chairs for 30 students, and I think I had 42. And there was an oil heater in the classroom. And every time the wind blew, the soot would come out of that thing and . . . float all around the room, everywhere. It was just filthy. And there was a high school class up, above me. They changed classes every 40 minutes, and they thundered down the stairs, and every time they changed, the tables and stuff, would scrape around upstairs. You know, it was grim.[27]

The Christmas Concert

Not all rural communities in British Columbia could be defined by the term as we often understand it. Many were communities in name alone. They were identified as such on maps of the province, but they were unremarkable in terms of having a core business or recreation area. Homesites were scattered, transportation was limited, and opportunities for socializing were infrequent. Yet they were communities, and many were connected by strong traditions surrounding their local events and activities.

My own experience as a rural teacher included a year as teaching principal at the three-teacher Devereaux Elementary School in the South Peace River area. The immediate 'community' consisted of the school, two teacherages, an ice house, and an outdoor rink. One or two nearby houses were the only other buildings visible in this region of woods and grain fields. As the days chilled and ponds in the area began to freeze, students who had played inside the boards of the rink during the summer and fall began to ask when the rink would be flooded for skating. I had no answer, and before I had an opportunity to pose the question to the school district's maintenance department, the answer arrived in the form of a delegation of parents asking the same question. Clearly, the responsibility was mine, at least in their eyes. Dutifully, I flooded the rink, working with a rubber hose in the early morning and during the evenings and weekends. The students watched with interest until the task was completed. I had done my job, and now it was time to skate.

In some communities, the school itself became a social centre. In areas with minimal opportunity for outings at the theatre, films borrowed by the teacher to run for students were also viewed by the community:

> Nobody had thought to order films. And you had to order them every four months, so they were kind of annoyed that I didn't show films about the second day. The parents came and said, "You've got a film projector, now are you going to show films?" . . . Whatever films I'd chosen to show the children, I then had to show that week on Friday evening at the school. I showed the films, and then they played Whist. They could play Whist until bloody two o'clock in the morning. I was so tired.[28]

Whether Whist, school films, or other community social activities, events in the rural area often carried their own unique local stamp. As John Robertson discovered in the small Elk Valley area that included the tiny communities of Natal, Michel, and Middletown in the space of less than half a mile, "It was really different, the dance hall. It's the first time I've ever been to a dance where there's actually real dogs in the dance hall."[29]

In many communities, the school's Christmas concert was a major annual event. The community's expectations were clear – concerts were primarily the responsibility of the teachers. The planning cycle was also clear, at least in local minds and in the memories of those assigned the task. For John Robertson, the end of the War in 1945 was a good thing, but it was also an event to be held in perspective against the sober realities of one's first Christmas concert:

> *Middle of September, a bunch of the mothers came down and said, "When are we going to start practising for the Christmas Concert?? I said, "You've got to be kidding! It's not the end of September yet." And I certainly wasn't musical. So I said, "I'll call you." So I think about the beginning of November we started on the Christmas Concert. And they got it all in shape.*
>
> *We had a practice the night before at the South Slocan Community Hall, and I had to walk down the railroad track. I was living at the staff house in South Slocan . . . The snow! There must have been ten feet of snow on either side of the railroad track, and I heard a train coming, and I seriously thought about not getting off the tracks. That rehearsal was just terrible! . . . It was dark, and I was walking home, and here's the train, and I thought, "I think I'll just stick right here." But it went fine . . .*
>
> *It was a different kind of a situation, because the teacher had been there had been there maybe 20 years, and they were due for a change. So I guess I was the change, and they were quite happy about that. They'd never had a man teacher in the school, I don't think. So we just had a great time.[30]*

The rural school Christmas Concert has been the focus of many pieces of writing, including letters home from beginning teachers, and concerts of various kinds are memories for many children. Clearly, these events also stand out in the minds of many teachers, especially if they include memories of having unwittingly challenged existing social norms. Marjorie (Thatcher) King recalled her initiation as a beginning teacher:

> *I remember being rather embarrassed, because we had been taught to do so and so, and there I was a very, very young*

teacher going into this community...I wanted desperately to do well. And I remember planning a Christmas concert, and it went very well. But somewhere I had had a communication problem with some people in the community. I don't remember how it happened now, but they volunteered to do something, and it was kind of like, we always do this, we've always done that, and so forth. And not knowing any better, I said, "Well, you don't have to do that, I can do it."

And I remember came the time for the concert . . . I must have asked one of the men who was the School Board Chairman . . . to do something. I remember him standing up on the stage . . . we didn't have a stage, it was on the platform, and then he stepped down, and I can still hear him saying, "I'm not really allowed up on the stage this year." I think it was this young whippersnapper of a teacher who had come in and changed the rules. I remember feeling quite embarrassed, but I survived . . . the people were very good to me.[31]

Some experiences were less comfortable. Holidays were a time to celebrate, and the tradition in a few places was to treat the concert as another celebration opportunity. The results were both surprising and disappointing to young Ken Bradley, who as a beginning teacher in 1927 was dismayed by a local concert that was far different than what he had been taught at the Normal School:

My first Christmas Concert disgusted me so much that I went to Prince Rupert next Christmas, and the Christmas after . . . Everybody was drunk but me . . . I mean, one young man picked up his father and took him to the door of the schoolhouse and threw him out into four feet of snow. That's the kind of thing they did. To me, that's not Christmas business. We . . . learned that Christmas Concert idea from the Music teacher at Normal, Miss Riddell.[32]

The School Inspector

Whether or not the inspector came to the school, and the nature of the visit if he (always "he") did, was dependent on several factors, weather and travel complexities among them. But they did visit, often with memorable effect, though the content and focus of their visits and comments varied. For many, though, the inspector's visits were a source of memories, even encouraging one's vocabulary development:

> *About the only good report I had was when the Inspector thought my presence on the playground had a salutary effect, and I had to go and look it up in the dictionary, to see what "salutary effect" meant.*[33]

As a young graduate, John Jackson was admonished by the inspector to "Watch your blackboard writing." He recalled, "And after that ... I got compliment after compliment on my blackboard writing."[34] Not all were admonished. In some cases, the visit was marked both by the teacher's uncertainty and the inspector's complete non-intrusion. John Robertson was first panicked, then bemused by his first visit from an inspector:

> *About the middle of October, he came out to my one-room school, introduced himself, said that he would like to stay for the morning, and sat in the back, in the desk. Never lifted his head up the whole time. All he did was write for two and a half hours.*
>
> *I thought, "Oh, God, I wonder where I'm going to be teaching in December, January." About twenty to twelve, he said, "I've got to go now. I had to find someplace where I wasn't going to be disturbed. I've got a speech to give to the Kiwanis today at noon." He never did come back.*
>
> *So when I applied for Trail, you had to have a copy of your Inspector's report . . . So I phoned him up and said . . . "I just applied for a job in Trail and I need an Inspector's Report." He said, "Okay, I'll write a letter of reference."*[35]

Some memories of the inspectors were more positive, perhaps almost the epitome of what Bill Cross (1949-50) thought should be the role of the authoritative classroom visitor:

> *I was lucky, because my first superintendent was Bill Plenderleith, and he was an absolutely marvelous superintendent at bringing on new teachers. He was a non-disturbing presence in your classroom. He'd come in, he didn't take the classroom over or anything.*
>
> *He'd ask if he could sit in the back for a little while . . . he was always the gentleman, and he would ask if he could take a couple of kids out in the hallway to read and talk to them. And then he'd come in, and after his first visit, he would go away*

and say, "I'll come back in a couple," and he'd make an appointment, when was it convenient with you . . . and he recognized from my farm boy English background that I needed some help in teaching grammar and all . . . And he said, "I'll come, I'll teach the first day's, and then you teach the rest of them through and tell me how it goes." Not, "I'm going to come and watch you teach them." He was quite a guy. And I got onto very good terms with Bill Plenderleith.[36]

Making a Life

The richness of the interviewees' stories was particularly evident when they spoke of their lives beyond the classroom. In some instances, the boundaries between work life and social/ recreational life were blurred, often because of the teacher's involvement outside school with students, parents, and community. Joe Lott recalled that he and his classmates had been somewhat prepared for independent living by a perceptive Normal School instructor who realized what lay ahead for many of her students:

She taught a sort of a homemaking class, and we were taught to darn socks, and put buttons on clothing, and make simple meals, et cetera, because the reality of it was we were all going to go out to little teacherages or bachelor accommodation or whatever, somewhere in the backwoods of BC. You did not expect to get into the big cities for several years when you first started.[37]

For many of these graduates, surviving and succeeding was a matter of practicing, of making do with what was available, and of living with the realization that in social terms at least, things were not always perfect. Young men such as Pat Floyd were sometimes aided by their more experienced colleagues. He recalled:

I had an apartment above the Post Office. I started to do my own cooking because it had a kitchen facility. It was a bachelor suite, but some of the older members of the staff said, "That's not good enough." And so, they talked, first of all to one lady - she did it for a while until her health [wouldn't let her] carry on, and then to another woman, both of whom ran boarding homes, to take me on as an extra meal, for my lunch

*and dinner. I did breakfast at home, in the apartment . . . The
second place where I went there were . . . other teachers
staying there. So we just carried on our social life. And that
was our social life, was the group of teachers. That's really all
there was in this town . . . very frustrating for a young male.
There were no eligible females. Anybody who was a girl, was
in high school. When they hit 18, 19, they left.[38]*

In many cases, British Columbia's rural communities were also
economically poorer communities, where a new teacher was
prized as a possible source of rare extra income. Local politics and
power probably played a role in some decisions regarding
selection and assignment of living places. Not every one of these
could be considered a commodious 'home away from home.' The
story of one 1926-27 graduate was recounted by her daughter:

*The man was the Superintendent of Schools and five of the
seven kids came from that family, and she had to share a bed
with two of the girls. And then the weather came through the
boards of the siding of the house. If it rained, it rained on
them. She got the part of the bed next to the wall because
they knew that whoever slept there got rained on.[39]*

That was not her mother's only experience with living
arrangements that afforded little comfort and even less privacy.
Apparently:

*Mom boarded in one place where there were holes in the floor
boards . . . she discovered that the man of the house would
stand underneath (the house was dark, she had the lamp on to
get ready for bed) and look up through the floor boards while
she was changing.[40]*

Experiences with cracks in the floor, knotholes, and too-large
spaces around chimney pipes probably contributed to a good deal
of discomfort and embarrassment for young teachers being
introduced to a new community. Doubtless they remembered the
admonishments of their Normal School instructors regarding
modesty and good behaviour:

*But some of the experiences were unbelievable. A woman
expected to share a double bed with the older daughter, or not
so older daughter. Taking a bath in the tub in the kitchen. The
stovepipe went through and of course there's a nice opening
around the stovepipe going through, and the other children*

would be there . . . [they] giggled seeing the teacher having a bath in the pan in the kitchen. In some cases . . . this month you board with us, next month, you go there, next month, you'll go there. They were sharing the wealth. The teacher paid for her board and lodging, but you changed your accommodation each month to satisfy.[41]

Sometimes, the experience was neither embarrassing nor uncomfortable. It was just closer than a young person beginning both a career and an independent adult life would enjoy. Often, though, there was little choice for young men such as Ken Bradley:

I boarded with one of the families. In fact, I had most of my students living in the same house . . . So I had them 24 hours a day, seven days a week . . . I stayed with the same one . . . three years.[42]

Often, teachers would have the satisfaction of acting informally as adult educators in the community, although sometimes the pleasure was the vicarious enjoyment of an onlooker, not the joy of directly helping an adult learn to read:

And there was hardly one of the people, the heads of families, that had even been to high school . . . The lady at the house where I boarded could only read and write after her oldest daughter taught her . . . Because they used to sit around the table at night and I'd hear this woman trying to read Eaton's catalogue, and she'd be picking out words here and there. They didn't have much.[43]

Occasionally rural residents, in one case Marjorie (Campbell) Brown's landlord, secured sources of income that placed them in a secure position, but only as long as their enemies were few and law enforcement was far away:

At Tofino . . . liquor was being taken across to the States. And the place where I stayed, he was a bootlegger . . . was quite common, he had a very low, very fast boat. You could almost tell that was going to be a liquor-runner, nothing else . . . He was a rum-runner.[44]

Sometimes, opportunities arose to contribute to family finances. Custodial arrangements varied among schools, and some responses were both creative and well received by parents:

There was no custodian. The School Board gave us $15 a month to spend on custodial work. So we used to divide it up between the kids, who'd sign on for a week or two. And, of course, the bigger boys got to pack the wood and the water, the little kids got smaller amounts, and did chalkboards and brushes and stuff like that. And they were all happy as anything to get a dollar at the end of the month.[45]

Often, especially in tiny communities, the teacher was one of the few with a secure income. In the early years, even that was not always assured. In some instances, the rural teacher's salary was paid in part by the local school board, the balance by the Department of Education. The salary, even though it was not abundant, was much appreciated by these young teachers:

Paid ten months – once a month, I got a cheque for $90.00. I felt lucky. My rent was $23 a month for the little house.[46]

Beyond the classroom, beyond the variable joys of independent living, these teachers built their lives. For many, either because of their natural inclinations and interests or as a function of climate and surroundings, the outdoors was an integral and enjoyable part of those lives:

I walked around, and the second year, I thought it would be fun to file on a quarter section of land, which I did. And, it's nice to walk along the roads, you know, a half mile, and say, "That's mine"... And then before I quit and went home, I abandoned it. But it was fun. And then on Saturday, I always walked out to get the mail ... Eight miles to the railway station, and five miles down the track.[47]

For some, recreation was less solitary. Many enjoyed the recreational opportunities enabled by the climate of the province's rural interior:

In McBride, it's very cold in the winter, so there were a lot of winter activities. The fellow who taught Phys. Ed. and I did a lot of hiking together, a bit of skiing. He was a very good skier, and I was not, I was a total novice, but we went skiing together. A bit of skating, bob-sledding. Basically, it was all winter activities.[48]

Rural teachers were often admonished by their Normal school instructors and by others to maintain a certain distance from the community. It was important, they were told, to avoid the possibility of community divisiveness or allegations of favoritism. Bill Cross applied a creative twist to socializing within his multi-ethnic community:

> The men would often invite me to go and have a beer at the pub, and on Friday afternoons I'd go to the Wheat Sheaf and have one glass of beer, because I could meet the Scots population. And then I would go to the other beer parlour, at Cassidy, have one glass of beer, because I could meet the Yugoslav guys. And I alternated my Fridays . . . So, they'd get a Vancouver Island farm boy in there, they felt quite happy. And so I gradually got the people together by working with the men.[49]

Sometimes a teacher's involvement in recreation, extracurricular activities, and service to the community had a particular flavour because of his or her particular skills. Marjorie (Campbell) Brown introduced the children of Lac la Hache to swimming, an activity they might otherwise have missed even with a lake at the front door:

> We generally had Christmas concerts, but outside of that, there wasn't anything. But, when I went up to Lac La Hache, here they had a lake at their front door. And I taught all the kids to swim, and they swam well by the time I was through, because I liked to swim, taught all the kids to swim.[50]

Marjorie also enjoyed her introduction to another typical country activity, horseback riding. That pursuit, though new and highly enjoyable, was not entirely uneventful. She recalled her initiation into one of the favourite pursuits of people living in the Cariboo region:

> I think I enjoyed my horseback riding more than anything. We couldn't get anywhere if we couldn't ride a horse, and I had never ridden a horse. So, anyway, the fellow that I eventually married, he bought me a horse and all the trappings, and I went all over. And then I went visiting one night. And I expected that whoever it was had tightened up my cinch enough, but they hadn't.
>
> Coming home, I got about half way home, I guess, I had been carrying my hat because it had been almost too warm to wear it . . . good joke. I thought, "It's getting a big chilly," and I went to put it on, expecting my saddle to stay where it was,

but my saddle didn't, and I went off. And I can remember saying to myself, "If my arm didn't hurt, I'd feel just all right." And that's what I was saying to myself all the way home, "If my arm didn't hurt, I'd feel just all right." I had broken my arm. They took me up to Williams Lake and I went into hospital there and they put it into a cast.[51]

Kay (Kennedy) Hinkes (VPNS 1945-46), who taught for many years in the South Cariboo community of Clinton, was no stranger to horses. That fact enabled her to foil the efforts of some of her students to play a trick on their new teacher:

Naturally, there were the mischievous Grade 5 boys. Here is one incident they schemed to test this teacher from the city: "Would you like to go riding on Saturday?" I agreed. Saturday came with both boys on horses and leading one for me. Eagerly they watched as I mounted the animal. Yes, it crow-hopped and bucked. Much to the boys' dismay, I rode the brute to a standstill and laughed. After only four days of teaching, I won the respect of my pupils because I could ride and thought it a good joke. No one knew I had grown up on a farm and had ridden horses since I was a wee tot.[52]

Kay's description of her Cariboo riding adventure offers a delightful capsule comment to capture the essence of other Victoria Provincial Normal School graduates' experiences. Many could say of the careers they began during the period from 1915 to 1956, and of their adventures and misadventures along the way, "I rode the brute to a standstill and laughed."

For these teachers, the "brute" assumed many forms: succeeding in the practicum experience, organizing a multi-grade classroom, 'making do' with less-than-superb facilities, learning about rural realities, and helping struggling pupils to read. As I learned during the interviews, at the end of their careers many of these teachers looked back on years of satisfying engagement with students, parents, and communities, "and laughed" with the same deep pleasure Kay (Kennedy) Hinkes had felt on the day she realized she had passed the test.

The end of this chapter also marks the end of an era. British Columbia's Normal Schools closed in 1956, merged into the province's college and university system. That year, the Victoria Provincial Normal School joined Victoria College en route to becoming, seven years later in 1963, the Faculty of Education at the new University of Victoria. Its graduates carried away both their memories of the building constructed in 1915 to serve the work of preparing teachers for the elementary classrooms of British Columbia and their legacy of friendship and camaraderie with their fellow travellers.

Notes to Chapter 7

1 Lorraine Johns to Lillian Anderson, ca. 1922, BCA MS 2796.
2 Lillian Williams (Anderson) to BCA from, date unknown, BCA MS 2796.
3 Marjorie (Campbell) Brown 2002.
4 Ken Bradley 2002.
5 Marjorie (Thatcher) King 2003.
6 Dorothy (Millner) Robertson 2002.
7 Ibid.
8 Joe Lott 2002.
9 Ibid.
10 Ken Bradley 2002.
11 Percy Wilkinson 2002.
12 Ken Bradley 2002.
13 John Jackson 2002.
14 Anne (Daser) Walters 2002.
15 Kay (Kennedy) Hinkes, "1945-46 Alumni Victoria Provincial Normal School: Some of our stories," in principal researcher's file.
16 John Robertson 2002.
17 Ibid.
18 Pat Floyd 2002.
19 Marjorie (Thatcher) King 2003.
20 Joe Lott 2002.
21 John Jackson 2002.
22 Bill Cross 2002.
23 Joe Lott 2002.
24 Marjorie (Thatcher) King 2003.
25 Ibid.
26 Norma (Matthews) Mickelson 2002.
27 Ibid.
28 Bill Cross 2002.
29 John Robertson 2002.
30 Ibid.
31 Marjorie (Thatcher) King 2003.
32 Ken Bradley 2002.
33 Percy Wilkinson 2002.
34 John Jackson 2002.
35 John Robertson 2002.
36 Bill Cross, interview by Vernon Storey, 15 July 2002, interview 22, transcript in interviewer's file.
37 Joe Lott 2002.
38 Pat Floyd, interview by Vernon Storey, 9 August 2002, interview 14, transcript in interviewer's file.
39 Dr. Diana (Lee) Mitchell, interview by Vernon Storey, 5 November 2002, interview 11a, transcript in interviewer's file.
40 Ibid.
41 Percy Wilkinson 2002.
42 Ken Bradley 2002.
43 Ibid.
44 Marjorie (Campbell) Brown 2002.
45 Anne (Daser) Walters 2002.
46 Marjorie (Campbell) Brown 2002.
47 Ken Bradley 2002.
48 Pat Floyd 2002.
49 Bill Cross 2002.
50 Marjorie (Campbell) Brown 2002.
51 Ibid.
52 Kay (Kennedy) Hinkes, ibid.

LEARNING TO TEACH
TEACHER PREPARATION
IN VICTORIA, BC
1903-1963

Chapter 8
Endnote:
After Forty Years

The formal training of teachers in British Columbia began in 1901 with the opening of the Vancouver Provincial Normal School. The primary focus of this book, though, has been on the Victoria Provincial Normal School, which opened in the capital city in 1915. The years from 1901 to 1956 are sometimes remembered by teachers and teacher educators in British Columbia, and by historians interested in the record, as the "normal school days." During that period, several of western Canada's universities were established. Approaches to teacher preparation had changed across North America, and the pre-service phase was increasingly being regarded as a mainstream post-secondary education activity to be housed in colleges and universities.

The pattern of development in British Columbia differed somewhat from that of other settings. Unlike trends elsewhere, in British Columbia the normal schools did not become four-year teacher's colleges, despite then-vice-principal Harry Gilliland's 1953 proposals prefaced by his observation that:

1. Much of the success of recruitment depends upon the prestige of the agents doing the recruiting and of the institution they represent.

(a) Each Normal School should be renamed a Teachers' College.
(b) Its teaching staff should be called a Faculty – just as is the teaching staff of the Summer School of Education.
(c) The salaries of the senior faculty members should be

commensurate with the great importance of the work they do.
(d) Senior members of the Faculty should be honoured in the same way as Directors and Inspectors by being placed on the senior invitation list for invitations to important public functions.[1]

Whether or not the work of preparing teachers subsequently received the "commensurate" remuneration and honour called for by Harry Gilliland is a matter of individual perspective. However, the disciplined study of teaching would soon be formally incorporated into the work of British Columbia's higher education institutions, first as a college department and then as a university faculty, in the case of the Victoria School.

The decision to close both Provincial Normal Schools was confirmed by the provincial government in May, 1956, and the responsibility for elementary teacher preparation was assigned to the University of British Columbia:

This year marks the end of an era of teacher-training in this Province, and September will see the beginning of a new organization under the College of Education of the University of British Columbia. The period when elementary teachers received their academic and professional education in normal schools has come to an end . . . Under the new College of Education at the University of British Columbia elementary teachers will be given teaching certificates after two years of the Bachelor of Education degree program, or in some cases after a one-year emergency program. They will be encouraged to continue by summer sessions, or by winter sessions, toward the completion of the Bachelor of Education degree. Secondary-school teachers will be trained in a five-year Bachelor of Education degree program.[2]

The move to bring teacher education into the university system occurred in Canada later than elsewhere:

After the First World War, in the United States there was a rapid trend for the one-year normal schools to develop into junior colleges, and later into degree-granting teachers' colleges, which in some cases also gave liberal arts degrees. Parallel with this was a further development: the recognized universities of the United States began establishing on their campuses faculties or colleges of education, so that today

[1956] all teacher-training in the United States is given either in degree-granting teachers' colleges or the universities, and over half the States demand a four-year degree for the elementary teaching certificate.[3]

The move sparked little controversy among the final group of students at the Victoria Provincial Normal School. They had been sharing 'their' facilities with Victoria College for ten years, and they realized both the inevitability and the significance of the change. Further, they were only at the School for one year. Pat Floyd, a member of the 1956 class, commented:

When we entered that year in Normal School, we were all aware that this would be the last year where you could take teacher training after grade 12 and then go directly into teaching. The following year, I think the minimum was two years. And it was known that the members of the faculty of the Normal School would, by and large, all become members of the College faculty . . . Victoria College at that time was still a component of UBC, really . . . [in] the newspaper . . . at the end of the year that we graduated, there's a picture of some of the faculty . . . walking down the stairs, and they were going out as teachers of the Normal School and becoming professors of the new Victoria College [Division] of Teacher Education.[4]

Pat would eventually return to work at the Lansdowne campus, during another period that marked transition and development in post-secondary education in Victoria. In 1956, Victoria still did not have its own university, though Victoria College was affiliated with the University of British Columbia. Completing a degree in education meant for most a transfer to UBC and several years' attendance at night school and summer school.

In 1963, ending a struggle that had begun in the 1800s, the University of Victoria was inaugurated and established on its Gordon Head campus, a property unknown to Normal School graduates except as an army camp. Victoria College today has been replaced by its successor, the multi-campus and diverse Camosun College. Yet one marker of the early years of teacher preparation in British Columbia remains. The visitor can still see, carved in stone over the main front door of the edifice now refurbished and called the Young Building, the simple inscription 'Normal School.'

Notes to Chapter 8

[1] Harry Gilliland, "Suggestions for Recruitment," (Victoria, BC: University of Victoria Archives and Special Collections, AR 329, 1.22).

[2] *BCGN, 4:5*, May 1956, p. 8.

[3] Ibid.

[4] Pat Floyd 2002.

Aerial view of Lansdowne campus of Victoria Provincial Normal School after PNS closure, ca 1985. Photo courtesy of UVic Archives, reference # 007.0301.

LEARNING
TO TEACH
TEACHER PREPARATION
IN VICTORIA, BC
1903-1963

CHRONOLOGY

1872	*Bill 16 An Act Respecting Public Schools*; Provincial Board of Education created, Superintendent appointed (must be an experienced teacher certified elsewhere Section 4; creation of additional school districts authorized; Board authorized to examine and certify teachers.
1872, May 15-16	First teacher certification examinations.
1901	Vancouver Provincial Normal School opens.
1903	Victoria College (McGill) opened (first year arts and science courses); located at Victoria High School
1903-1915	Before the Victoria Provincial Normal School, there was no systematic teacher preparation in Victoria - Victoria College McGill was a typical pre-exam route to certification. On completion, a large proportion of these students became teachers.
1915	Victoria Provincial Normal School (VPNS) opened in new Young Building; D.L. MacLaurin Principal.
1915-1942	Victoria Provincial Normal School remains sole tenant of its dedicated building.
1915-1920	Victoria College closed, McGill College Vancouver opened.
1920, April 1	"The Victoria College, in Affiliation With

	the University of British Columbia" created; administratively separate from Vic High; practical authority vested in Dept. of Education; space allocated at Victoria High School.
1920	Victoria College reopens, in Craigdarroch Castle.
1925	Putman Weir *Survey of the School System* report.
1925-26	Principal MacLaurin on medical leave; Vernon L. Denton Acting Principal.
1926-27	J.W. Gibson Acting Principal; Principal MacLaurin returns mid-year.
1932	MacLaurin appointed Assistant Superintendent of Education; Vernon L. Denton appointed Principal of VPNS.
1942-1945	VPNS Building turned over to federal government as army hospital; VPNS housed briefly in Shrine Temple on View Street, then in Memorial Hall, Christ Church Cathedral.
1944	Principal Denton dies; H.O. English appointed VPNS Principal
1946-1956	Building shared with Victoria College (which left Craigdarroch).
1954	Principal English dies; Harry C. Gilliland appointed VPNS Principal.
1955	*Victoria College Act* merges VPNS with Victoria College
1956, Spring	Final session of VPNS concludes.
1958	Victoria College Council names "Heads of Departments;" Henry Gilliland appointed Professor and Director of Teacher Education (13 faculty).
1958	Victoria College Department of Teacher

	Education created; affiliation after Normal Schools was with University of British Columbia.
1961, May 29	First degrees from *University of British Columbia (Victoria College)*.
1963, January 18	Premier Bennett announces University of Victoria.
1963	University of Victoria begins operation.

Picture by Edward Goodall, used by permission of Richard Goodall.

LEARNING TO TEACH

TEACHER PREPARATION
IN VICTORIA, BC
1903-1963